The Meditation of the Sad Soul

THE LITTMAN LIBRARY OF JEWISH CIVILIZATION

EDITORS:

David Goldstein
Louis Jacobs

The Meditation of the Sad Soul

ABRAHAM BAR ḤAYYA

Translated and with an Introduction by

GEOFFREY WIGODER

ROUTLEDGE & KEGAN PAUL · LONDON

First published 1969
by Routledge & Kegan Paul Limited
Broadway House, 68–74 Carter Lane, London, E.C.4

Printed in Great Britain by Western Printing Services Ltd,
Bristol

Distributed by Oxford University Press
ISBN 0 19 710018 X

Contents

Introduction

ABRAHAM BAR HAYYA'S *Meditation of the Sad Soul* has been recognized as one of the minor classics of medieval Jewish philosophy ever since it was first published just over a century ago.[1] Chronologically, it was written after the works of Saadya and Solomon Ibn Gabirol; approximately contemporaneously with those of Baḥya Ibn Pakuda and Judah Halevi; and before the works of Abraham Ibn Daud, Maimonides and their successors. Common to all those writers was the all-pervading influence of Arabic philosophy, and even their knowledge of Greek philosophy came to them by way of the abbreviations and adaptations of Greek works made by Arab philosophers. But like Jewish philosophers in other ages, their prime objective was the harmonization of current philosophical thought with Jewish tradition. Their endeavour was to set the current rationalism within the perspective of Jewish thought and to show as far as possible that no fundamental contradiction was implied. Each age evolved its own methodology, from the far-fetched allegorization of Philo to the pure theological synthesis of modern Jewish thinkers. Even within medieval times, there were wide varieties of approach. Thus when the Hebrew original of Ibn Gabirol's *Source of Life* had been lost and only the Latin translation preserved, it never was thought that its author had been a Jew. This, however, was an exceptional case. Other Jewish medieval writings are so distinctive that their origin is unmistakable. This is certainly true of Abraham

[1] *Hegyon ha-Nefesh* (Leipzig 1860), edited by E. Freimann; introductions by Freimann and S. J. L. Rapoport.

I

bar Ḥayya's book which is pervaded not only with Jewish content but with the Midrashic approach and exegesis. Indeed— after the first short section—the philosophical content is frequently incidental and buried in its homiletical context. Once it is extracted and examined, Abraham bar Ḥayya emerges as a significant and sometimes original thinker of interest not only historically but even meaningfully for the modern reader.[1]

In one important respect, he differed from most of the other outstanding Jewish medieval philosophers—namely, that he wrote in Hebrew whereas the others wrote in Arabic and were known to subsequent Jewish generations only through translations. All the works of Abraham bar Ḥayya were written in a lucid Hebrew— often involving the coining of terminology which passed into the language—and not only in philosophy but in all the many subjects on which this versatile author wrote he must be regarded as a pioneer of Hebrew literature.

HIS LIFE

Very few hard facts have emerged regarding his life. What is known of his biography is largely a weaving together of odd pieces of information gleaned by a perusal of his writings. Thus the only place where he can be said with any degree of certainty to have resided is Barcelona. At the period when Abraham bar Ḥayya lived, Barcelona was ruled by Christian counts who were in the vanguard of the Christian wars against the Arabs in Spain. This, however, did not imply any remoteness from Arabic culture which remained influential even in the Christian zones of Spain. Catalonia in the tenth and eleventh centuries was the centre of considerable activity in the spheres of mathematical and scientific scholarship. In this intellectual ferment, Jews were prominent and excelled in mathematics, physics, astronomy, alchemy, geography, medicine and surgery. In Barcelona itself, there was a Jewish quarter from the beginning of the eleventh century and according to the Arab historian Al-Himyari Barcelona contained as many

[1] See Leon D. Stitskin's *Judaism as a Philosophy* (New York 1960) for a consideration of the contemporary relevance of Abraham bar Ḥayya's philosophy.

Jews as Christians. Moreover, this was not only a period of efflorescence in secular scholarship among Jews, but is known as a golden age in Jewish studies and creativity. All forms of literature flourished while Talmud study had received a major impetus by the advent of Isaac Alfasi from North Africa (epitomizing the shift in the centre of gravity of Jewish life from Babylonia and Northern Africa to the Iberian peninsula).

Against this promising background, Abraham bar Ḥayya[1] achieved eminence. Neither the date nor the place of his birth or death are known. Suggestions have been made that he was born in 1065 or 1070 but no evidence is forthcoming, and any attempt to formulate a date is sheer guesswork.

The only two references to his youth in his writings state that 'from my youth I have been a student of astronomy' and 'in my youth I was honoured by kings and princes'. These honours are probably indicated in the two titles by which he is called in various manuscripts—'Savasorda' and 'Nasi'. 'Savasorda' is a corruption of the Arabic 'saḥib-al-shurta' and seems to denote a high court official, although the precise nature of this office is not clear. It was probably a half-judiciary, half-civil position which Abraham bar Ḥayya may well have earned as a result of his mathematical and astronomical knowledge, his skill in surveying and his familiarity with languages. 'Nasi' was not an uncommon title (a document recording a sale of land in Barcelona in the year 1096 mentions a Rabbi Abraham bar Joseph ha-Nasi) and denotes an office within the Jewish community exercising a judiciary function, which could impose punishment and regulate communal taxation. Whereas the court title would have been conferred by the Count, the other would have been the exclusive concern of the Jewish community.

There are various references to his living in Barcelona and it was in Barcelona that he co-operated with the Christian Plato of Tivoli

[1] There are several pointers that his patronymic should be transliterated as 'Ḥayya' rather than the more familiar 'Ḥiyya'. Originating from 'Ḥayyim', Ḥayya would be the more logical form and is found in Greek transliteration as ἀεια while in Spanish documents of that time it is transliterated 'Aya'. It is also noteworthy that in the preliminary poem introducing his book 'The Secret of Intercalation', our author rhymes 'Ḥayya' with 'Zekhayya'.

3

(who was responsible for translating and transmitting the system of Ptolemy to the Latin world) in translating works from Arabic into Latin. The only known incident in Abraham bar Ḥayya's life was a clash with his fellow-townsman, the distinguished scholar Judah ben Barzillai, over the time of a wedding which Abraham proposed to postpone for astrological reasons. Judah rejected this motivation, leading Abraham to write a defence of astrology.

It appears that at some time Abraham visited France. In his lifetime, Provence was part of the domain of the Count of Barcelona and he may well have visited there. He mentions several times in his writings that he had firsthand knowledge of the land of 'Tzarefat'. For example, in the introduction to his recently-published *Encyclopaedia*,[1] he writes: 'I have not embarked on writing this book out of my own choice nor to acquire honour, but many of my distinguished contemporaries—whose advice I must accept—have persuaded me to do so because in all the land of Tzarefat there is not a single book on these subjects in Hebrew. Consequently according to their suggestion, I translated from Arabic works into Hebrew.' Some scholars have questioned whether 'Tzarefat' as used by Abraham bar Ḥayya refers to what is known as 'France' or whether it is 'Provence'.

Various attempts have been made to determine the date of his death. A manuscript of his geometrical work dated 1136 refers to him as 'of blessed memory' but these words could have been a latter addition. Plato of Tivoli cites him as a collaborator up to 1136 but does not mention him in connection with his translation of Ptolemy's *Quadripartitium* in 1138. The evidence is not conclusive but points to his death in approximately 1136.

HIS WORKS

Even in an age of encyclopaedic scholarship, the breadth of Abraham bar Ḥayya's knowledge and writings is impressive. The following is a list of works that he is known to have written:

1. *The Secret of Intercalation.* An explanation of calendrical

[1] *Yesodei ha-Tevunah u-Migdal ha-Emunah* (Madrid-Barcelona 1952), Hebrew text p. 10, edited by J. Millas y Vallicrosa.

4

reckoning, written in 1123. This work was often quoted by later authors and became a major source for its subject.

2. *Plane and Solid Geometry* written with the object of assisting in field measurement. It defines geometrical terms and proceeds to prove propositions, as well as describing measuring instruments. It was translated into Latin by Plato of Tivoli and introduced Arabic trigonometry and mensuration into the West.

3. *The Reckoning of Astral Motions.* A book on astronomy and intercalation, which was widely used for several centuries as an astronomical handbook.

4. *The Form of the Earth and the Structure of the Heavenly Orbs.* The first exposition of the Ptolemaic system in Hebrew. It became the chief source of geographical knowledge in Jewish literature and was translated into Latin in the sixteenth century.

5. *The Foundations of Understanding and the Tower of Faith.* An encyclopaedia whose subject-matter covers arithmetic, optics, geometry, music, astronomy, logic, natural sciences, politics and theology. Only a part of the work has survived and it seems that the book is a translation from Arabic, to which Abraham bar Ḥayya added his own paraphrases and explanations. His manuscript on music (in the Vatican library) may not be therefore an independent composition but a section of this encyclopaedia.

6. Astronomical and astrological tables.

7. *The Scroll of the Revealer.* An eschatological work written to determine the end of Time. Basing himself on Jewish tradition and on astrology, he reaches the conclusion that the Messiah will appear between 1136 and 1448 (the latter being the date for the resurrection of the dead). This book was widely read and quoted in subsequent centuries and its influence extended to kabbalistic circles, especially the medieval Jewish mystics in Germany. It also exerted considerable influence on Isaac Abarbanel, much of whose astrological knowledge and historiography is based on it.

8. *The Meditation of the Sad Soul,* dealing with ethical and philosophical problems supported by proofs adduced from the homiletic exegesis of Biblical passages. The main topics are: creation, repentance, good and evil and the saintly life. The second

and third of the four parts are based on the sections of the Prophetical Books read in the synagogues on the Day of Atonement. It is quoted less than his other works and had comparatively little effect on subsequent thinkers.

A responsum of the scholar Jedaiah Bedersi, who lived in Barcelona in the fourteenth century, refers to 'a work on ethics and Bible interpretation by Abraham bar Ḥayya called "The Definition of Man" ' and this has led scholars to postulate a lost work. I would, however, suggest that the reference is to *The Meditation of the Sad Soul*, a work on ethics and Bible interpretation which commences with a doxology and proceeds to speak of the 'definition of man'. In the absence of a title page, Bedersi would have named this book by its first distinctive phrase. The identical phrase occurs in the introduction to his encyclopaedia but the context is such that it could not be mistaken for the title of the work nor could the encyclopaedia be called 'a work on ethics and Bible interpretation'.

Apart from original works, Abraham bar Ḥayya translated El-Imrani's work on algebra *De horarum electionibus* from Arabic to Latin and collaborated in other scientific translations with Plato of Tivoli.

HIS PHILOSOPHY

(This description is based on the *Meditation of the Sad Soul* unless otherwise stated.)

1. *God*

Unlike many other medieval Jewish philosophers, such as Saadya and Baḥya, Abraham bar Ḥayya does not concern himself with proofs for the existence or unity or attributes of God. The existence of God is implicitly assumed and there is no hint that this existence could possibly be questioned. The unity of God and the fact that God is the Creator is apparent both from the structure of the universe and from the Bible (notably Deuteronomy iv.39). Writing on arithmetic in his encyclopaedia he refers to one as the basis of number, and says: 'This God is One. He is illimitable, His existence is necessary and there is no cause to His existence.' The wisdom of God can be further adduced from the structure of man, and this he connects with Job xix. 26 which says 'From my flesh shall I see God'.

Abraham bar Ḥayya takes Divine attributes for granted and often mentions them, although he does not attempt to list them. Thus he states that wisdom and authority are two attributes shared by man with God.[1] God is omniscient, knowing all human secrets; omnipresent, in the highest of holy places and with the most humble on earth; and omnipotent, responsible for evil as well as good. Through His attribute of kindness He created the world and gave its benefits to its inhabitants. The attribute of justice is demonstrated by the equitable distribution of good and evil in this world whereby the righteous gets his due reward and the wicked his due punishment. The attribute of charity is manifested by the granting of eternal life after death to those whose merits and faults in this world are equally balanced. An important verse for the comprehension of God is Isaiah lvii. 15 which states: 'Thus saith the High and Lofty One who dwelleth for ever, whose name is holy'. 'Height' is an absolute attribute of God but 'Loftiness' is relative in that it describes the position of God in relation to things of this world. The phrase 'who dwelleth for ever' shows that He is immutable and immovable. 'Whose name is holy' indicates that no other thing can approach His holiness.

Following rabbinical tradition, the Divine name *Adonay* (The Lord) is said to be used in conjunction with the attribute of kindness and mercy; and *Elohim* (God) with the attribute of justice.

The existence of the Will and Word of God are assumed. All things exist in God's thought as separate Matter and Form until synthesized by the Divine Will, while it is the Word of God which gives the Form the power to combine with Matter.

2. *Cosmogony*

God first created things to exist in potentiality. This is compared with the mental image formed by man before he makes something.[2] Abraham bar Ḥayya does not attempt to prove *creatio ex*

[1] *Scroll of the Revealer*, p. 54.   [2] ibid., p. 8.

nihilo but assumes it with the statement that 'All intelligent non-Jewish sages as well as all Jewish ones are unanimously of the view that all material and created things were formerly nothing and not-being'[1] and he states specifically that man was created from nothing.[2] He therefore commences his account of creation from the moment of the 'going-up of all created things, whether permanent substance or transient accidents, into Divine Thought to be established in potentiality'.[3] The origin of things so established in Divine Thought is not further considered. As there was no Time prior to the six days of creation, any precedence of material things in potentiality to the six days of creation cannot be a precedence in time but only in nature.[4] He defines a precedence of nature as when the latter thing only has its establishment in the earlier so that we can argue from the later to the earlier but not vice versa. After the six days of creation, it can be said that the potential precedes the actual temporally but on the other hand actuality precedes potentiality by a precedence of degree because were it not for actuality, the potential would never be realized and become known.[5]

Abraham bar Ḥayya cites Scriptures to prove his points and in this instance he takes the Hebrew root *bara* to mean creation in potentiality, and the verbs *asah* and *yatzar* for actualization[6] (although he himself is not always consistent in this usage). Creation in potentiality took place in the six days of creation and things existed in potentiality until actualized as a result of the advent of the Divine Word. The Forms of all things that would ever exist and the origins of all species were created at the very beginning and existed in Divine Thought until it was time for their actualization.[7] Nothing can come into actuality without first existing in potentiality, and indeed when we say a thing exists in potentiality the meaning is 'in the potentiality of emerging to actuality'.[8] Following the Aristotelians, Abraham bar Ḥayya states that things existing in potentiality can be divided into Matter, Form and Not-Being. In order to actualize them, God removes the Not-Being and joins the Form with the Matter. This

---

[1] ibid., p. 5. [2] ibid., p. 49. [3] ibid., p. 8. [4] ibid., p. 8.
[5] ibid., p. 9. [6] ibid., p. 15. [7] ibid., pp. 17, 54. [8] ibid., pp. 8, 15.

process is described in detail. Although Form can exist without Matter, it cannot be apprehended by the senses until it is joined with Matter. A thing that has Form benefits the world; whatever is useless or harmful lacks Form, e.g. darkness which is not a positive creation but is merely the absence of light (that possesses form).[1] Matter itself has neither permanence nor perceptibility, neither shape nor form—but it is capable of receiving shape and form. It is too weak to exist independently without form and Form has the power to clothe matter with any shape. Consequently there is only one Matter but there are many Forms. However, Matter, like Form, can be subdivided into two parts. Matter can be divided into (a) pure and clean Matter and (b) the dregs and sediment. Form is divisible into (a) closed and sealed Form and (b) hollow and open Form.

Creation is caused in the first place by the emanation of a light from a closed Form. Both parts of Form and Matter are created by God to exist in potentiality. Nearest to God—and furthest from the material world—is the closed and sealed Form which is too pure to combine with Matter. This is self-subsistent and immutable, being identified with the Light created on the first day, according to the Book of Genesis. This Form is that of celestial beings (angels etc.), souls and all forms which trace their derivation to the Upper World which is entirely Light.[2]

The upper world above the firmament is divided into five degrees or worlds of Light (corresponding to the five times where Light is mentioned in the first chapter of Genesis):

(a) The World of Wonderful Light, corresponding to the 'Divine Throne' described by the Rabbis. This has been revealed to angels, prophets and to Moses on Mount Sinai.

(b) The Divine World, corresponding to the rabbinic 'Holy Spirit'. This was revealed to Moses at the Ark of the Covenant, to angels on missions, and to the people of Israel at Mount Sinai.

(c) The World of Knowledge, which is wisdom and Torah. This is revealed to various categories of angels and is accessible to the righteous among men.

[1] ibid., p. 5.   [2] *Secret of Intercalation*, p. 25.

(*d*) The World of the Soul, corresponding to the Divine Spirit within each man. Its light shines on the righteous while the wicked remain in darkness.

(*e*) The World of Nature, where Light is stored for the righteous in the world to come.

Light is thus not merely a symbol of Good or of the Upper World, but constitutes a definite metaphysical principle.[1] This is an essential feature of Neo-Platonic thought expounded by Plotinus and influencing Christian and Arab thought.[2] A Jewish tradition of Light evolved independently of Neo-Platonism. Starting with the Bible, and developed by the rabbis Light is taken as a great good and as a symbol for the Divine but is not considered suprasensibly. In Midrashic thought darkness has an independent existence, unlike the Platonic tradition according to which darkness is the absence of light. Jewish philosophers before Abraham bar Ḥayya drew from both the Neo-Platonic and Jewish traditions. Thus Saadya's doctrine of light[3] is more rabbinic than Neo-Platonic, and the philosopher closest in this respect to Abraham bar Ḥayya is Ibn Gabirol. Abraham bar Ḥayya's doctrine of light comprises Neo-Platonic elements, which can be traced back from Ibn Gabirol to Plotinus[4] although Stitskin connects this doctrine of Light with the Aristotelian 'separate intelligence'. In the next aspects of creation a splendour emanates from within the closed Form to shine on the hollow open Form, qualifying it to combine with Matter. The hollow, open Form now subdivides into two. One part joins the pure, clear Matter and from this juncture are formed the firmaments which exist perpetually in an unchangeable Form. The other part of the open Form joins the dregs and sediments of the Matter to form the bodies of this world—viz. the four elements and their various permutations. The corporeal world consists of: (*a*) Bodies

---

[1] *Scroll of the Revealer*, p. 22.

[2] The doctrine of metaphysical light reached Arab philosophers through such works as the so-called *Theology of Aristotle* and Pseudo-Empedocles.

[3] *Beliefs and Opinions* (Leipzig 1859), pp. 34, 66, 169.

[4] The Manichees spoke of five realms of light corresponding to sense, reason, thought, imagination and intention. As Abraham bar Ḥayya refers to Mani (*Scroll of the Revealer*, p. 22) it is possible that he may have known of this doctrine.

that do not change their form, i.e. the fixed stars. (*b*) Bodies that change their forms, but not their mass, i.e. elements. (*c*) Bodies that change their forms and their mass, i.e. plants.

The Divine Word now again causes the Light to emanate from the closed, sealed Form and it spreads over the firmament from point to point causing that Form already attached to Matter to change its place—hence the bodies of the moving stars. From this Light emanates a splendour which touches the body that changes its form and from this come the three types of living beings corresponding to the three elements in which life is possible (i.e. excluding fire) and embodying the three types of motion namely, swimming (water), flying (air), and going on foot (earth). The fourth type of motion is celestial, namely circular revolution which encompasses all existing things. In celestial bodies, the junction of Form and Matter is permanent and any change is merely that of position. Terrestrial bodies can change their Form, with or without altering their position.

Form can exist in four ways, and this can be expounded in rabbinical as well as philosophical terminology. Put philosophically, he makes the division into:

(*a*) Form that can exist on its own, without Matter, as in the Upper World;

(*b*) Form that is attached permanently to Matter, as in the firmament and stars;

(*c*) Form that revolves from body to body without ever returning to the Pure Form of the Upper World—as in earthly creatures;

(*d*) Form that is attached to Matter but only temporarily and after separating, returns to Pure Form—viz. the soul.

In rabbinical language, the division is into:

(*a*) Things that exist in this world and in the world to come—viz. light;

(*b*) Things that exist in this world but not in the world to come—viz. the firmament and luminaries;

(*c*) Things that exist neither in this world nor in the world to come —viz. lower creatures;

(*d*) What exists in the world to come, but without permanence in this world—viz. man.

The relation of matter and form had been discussed by philosophers since the time of Aristotle. The characteristic dichotomy of form and matter in Neo-Platonic thought is derived from Plotinus. The Arabic version of this in the so-called 'Theology of Aristotle' bears a certain resemblance to this doctrine of Abraham bar Hayya. However, Abraham's teaching cannot be identified exactly with any of his predecessors or contemporaries. It is in the tradition of post-Plotinian Neo-Platonism but differs, for example, from Ibn Gabirol to whom otherwise there are very strong resemblances. In certain details, Abraham prefers the views of the School of Arab Neo-Platonists, the Brethren of Purity, and other Arab philosophers. Abraham's works are not meant specifically for philosophers and this involved certain simplifications. Moreover, it would seem that the intention to relate his cosmogony homiletically with the first chapter of Genesis may also have led to modifications.

He concludes his account of creation by defining man as a rational living being, and postulating the familiar division of terrestrial objects into minerals, vegetables, animals and man. Each type received whatever faculties were required for self-fulfilment but only man is punished for not realizing his faculties.

There are important features of Abraham's cosmogony which emanate in Aristotelian thought. They include not only the conception of Matter and Form, but also potentiality and actuality. The concept of God as the Supremely Actual bringing the world, originally potential, into actual existence has also its basis in Aristotle (cf. *Physics*, 203.b.12). On the other hand creation as a system of emanation, irradiation and reversion to source is essentially the Plotinian system developed throughout all subsequent Neo-Platonic thought, and many ideas found in the first chapter of the *Meditation of the Sad Soul* can be traced back to the thought of Plotinus. But the differences must also be noted. Thus Abraham's system is not entirely emanational. Form and Matter are created by God and only associate when influenced by a Light which emanates from the Upper World; Form and Matter are not emanations but creations. Another difference is that Abraham maintains that creation took place in time, whereas for Plotinus, creation is timeless.

Abraham's order of creation should be compared with that of the Brethren of Purity who distinguished nine stages: 1. God—the Creative Spirit; 2. Reason—which is Pure Light containing the Forms of every thing; 3. The World Soul; 4. Universal Matter, which is spiritual; 5. Second Matter, i.e. the matter of corporeal beings; 6. The World of the Spheres; 7. Nature; 8. The elements of the sublunar world; 9. Products, viz. minerals, plants and animals.

Abraham bar Ḥayya starts with God, followed by Pure Light which also is Pure Form, thus containing also the third stage of the Brethren of Purity's system. He continues with universal and second matters, which do not however derive from Form but are coexistent. Then from the various combinations there are the World of the Spheres, elements and their products.

However, Abraham bar Ḥayya introduces some specifically Jewish elements into his sytem. The biblical account starts: 'God created' and this remained the starting-point for any Jewish account of creation. There is an interesting parallel to Abraham's views in Philo's *De Opificio Mundi* which states that the Incorporeal World is first firmly settled in Divine Reason and then created. The doctrine of the Divine attributes in Abraham bar Ḥayya is also essentially Jewish. He synthesizes Midrashic elements with the philosophical account of creation. Thus he starts with the Midrashic idea of the ascension of things into Thought (cf. *Genesis Rabbah* i. 4) and relates it to the philosophical account of the pre-existence of things in potentiality. Similarly he uses the emanational account of creation as a basis for his own exposition which is also founded on the fundamental religious idea of God as the creator.[1]

3. Time and Space

Time is an expression of the duration of things in existence. If nothing exists, there is no time, and similarly there was no Time

[1] Many parallels can also be drawn with the cosmogony contained in the *Reflections on the Soul* by Pseudo-Baḥya.

13

when all things were merely potential without being actualized. When all things were potential, so was Time, which was actualized with the first Divine fiat.[1] In his book on intercalation, Abraham bar Ḥayya states that there is no measure of Time apart from the reckoning of the celestial motions.[2] The assertion of some non-Jews that Time is eternal and that the world had no beginning is a denial of religious fundamentals and, in fact, constitutes a limitation of God.

The finiteness of Time is an essential principle. Not only must Time have had a beginning but it must also reach an end and this is the justification for eschatology. The book *Scroll of the Revealer* is an investigation into the end of time. When things will cease to go out to actuality, Time will have an end.[3]

Elsewhere he states[4] that things of this world are constituted of Form, Absence-of-Form and Time. Nothing exists in this world to which Time is not attached[5] and nothing—substance or accident—can exist, except in Time.[6] Thus Time is dependent on existing things. It has not Form because it cannot be perceived by the bodily senses; neither has it Absence-of-Form inasmuch as no Form can be imposed upon it and hence cannot be considered as absent from it.[7] However, both Form and Absence-of-Form depend upon Time and cannot exist apart from it. So Time has neither Form nor Absence-of-Form but is joined to all created things, and all created things are in it. These include light and darkness (i.e. day and night) which are not themselves Time but exist in Time like all other created Things.[8]

Time has no permanency. Time-Past is Not-Being; Time-Future is Potential. Time rolls on, unapprehended by the corporeal senses, because it has no Form. It can only be apprehended intellectually. It is not *in* another thing but is always *attached* to the other thing and dependent on it.[9]

Body is that which has width, breadth and depth attached to a thing of magnitude. Space is defined as that which envelops the shape of the body all round from the outside. Thus the transparent

[1] *Scroll of the Revealer*, p. 10.   [2] *Secret of Intercalation*, p. 3.
[3] *Scroll of the Revealer*, p. 10.   [4] ibid., p. 16.   [5] ibid., pp. 7–8.
[6] Ibid., pp. 7–8.   [7] ibid., p. 6.   [8] ibid., p. 8.   [9] ibid., p. 8.

14

light of the first day is space to the firmament as it surrounds it on all sides. This transparent light—otherwise, the closed and sealed Form—does not itself need space to surround it but can serve as the space for another body.

4. *Man*

Man is the summit of creation, the highest and most complex of all creatures. Through his possession of reason (=wisdom) he is distinguished from all other creatures. This distinction is expressed by (i) the special command for his creation in Genesis; (ii) the Divine Spirit within him; and (iii) the Divine command granting him domination over other living creations.

Man is defined as the Rational Living Being. Living Being is any mortal body which grows. Rational is the power of reason to apprehend intellectually and to make moral distinctions. Man is distinguished from animals by the possession of this rational faculty as well as by the power of speech. He can moreover apprehend and even participate in certain aspects of Divine wisdom.[1] In his corporeal faculties, man is like animals; but spiritually, he resembles angels and creatures of the upper world.[2] Man resembles angels, for example, in his knowledge of good and evil but he differs from them in that he is affected by good and evil (whereas angels cannot be reached by evil).[3]

Man's soul is equated with that Form which is temporarily attached to Matter, but ultimately returns to Pure Form. The human soul can be healthy or sick, alive or dead. Its health is wisdom; its sickness, folly. Its life is the fear of God and the performance of good deeds; its death the performance of wickedness. The most perfect type of soul is that which has health and life, and this is the soul of the man who separates himself from all aspects of this world for the sake of the world to come. His fate is to be completely emancipated from matter and to return to the Upper World of Pure Form. If the soul has both health and death—i.e. man who combines wisdom with wickedness—it will not be able to emancipate itself completely from matter but will remain in the subsolar universe—although above the sublunar—

[1] ibid., p. 54.   [2] ibid., p. 55.   [3] ibid., p. 61.

without attaining the Upper World of Light. If the soul has sickness and life, i.e. the pious but foolish man, it will at first free itself from matter but as it remains in the sublunar world it will eventually become reattached to matter, and this process of transmigration will continue until it eventually acquires the requisite wisdom to enable it to ascend to the upper world. Abraham bar Ḥayya criticizes Aristotle for the statement that forms and souls revolve in the world but do not return to their original matter, because matter is essentially formless—and when it loses the form, it loses its identity. His criticism is that God can recognize matter and He can bring any soul or form back to the matter to which it was originally attached.[1] Finally if the human soul has sickness and death, it perishes completely, like beasts and animals.

Elsewhere[2] he describes five types of death. Firstly there is the death of the wicked heathen without wisdom, fear of God or Torah. This death is complete perdition, like that of beasts or animals. Next is the death of those who go down to Gehinnom to undergo everlasting punishment. This is the death of wicked non-Jews, who have wisdom but no Torah, and of unrepentant Jewish apostates. Thirdly, there is the death of those who have on the one hand merits, but on the other guilt for which they have not atoned. They first must expiate their guilt and only thereafter are permitted to enter Paradise. Fourthly, there is the death of the righteous who go straight to Paradise. Finally there are those, like Elijah, who are privileged to enter Paradise without dying.

5. The Soul

Man possesses three faculties or souls—the vegetative soul, by which he grows; the animal or vital soul, by which he moves; and the rational soul. The vegetative soul is the soul by which man eats, drinks and propagates—in which actions he resembles plants. The animal soul is the source of emotions and of motion, which man shares with animals. The rational soul brings man to the fear of God and the observance of the commandments which ensure him the life of the world to come.[3]

The three names for the soul in Genesis are: 'living soul'

[1] ibid., pp. 50–1.   [2] ibid., pp. 109–10.   [3] ibid., p. 58.

(Genesis ii. 7), 'breath of life' (Genesis vi. 17) and 'spirit of life' (Genesis ii. 7). The first two terms apply to the animal soul. All four types of living thing—fish, fowls, animal and man—possess the 'living soul' and all, except fish, possess the 'breath of life'. Only man, however, is endowed with the 'spirit of life' which is breathed into him by God and corresponds to the rational soul.

The proper way of life is for the vegetative and animal souls to be subdued to the rational. If the rational soul rules, man is pure and perfect; if he lets his rational soul be dominated by his animal soul, he is evil and wicked. In most men, there is constant conflict between the rational and animal souls. If neither prevails, he will be the average man; if the rational soul prevails, he will be a good man; and if the animal soul predominates, he will be a wicked man.

At death, man loses his vegetative and animal souls, but retains his rational soul, the 'spirit of life' which receives reward or punishment for his deeds. The animal soul has neither merit nor guilt. Death cannot touch the 'spirit of life' but when it leaves the body, the body dies—the animal soul perishing completely as in the death of animals or evil men.[1] The rational soul is emancipated from this world, which it regards as a prison and where it has no pleasure but it is consoled by the reward of the world to come. The biblical phrase 'thou shalt afflict thy soul' refers to the affliction of the animal soul by withholding it from worldly and carnal thoughts so that the rational soul will be apart from the world and can contemplate the holiness of the Upper World. Worship of God is by the rational soul when it is entirely occupied with the fear of God.

6. The saint (ḥasid)

As stated in the description of Abraham bar Ḥayya's doctrine of man, the highest type of individual is the soul having health and life, i.e., the soul of the man who separates himself from this world. The essential characteristic of this man is his aloofness from all the affairs of this world and his devotion to the world to come

[1] ibid., p. 59.

and the fear and worship of God. The life of such a man is described as a perpetual Sabbath and his pleasure is defined as the meditation on the laws of God. He restrains his mouth, his hands and his heart from any activity that is not for the glory of God. God grants him spiritual reward for his conduct; this man's prayer will be answered and he will be spared from all trouble. These true believers can be divided into three groups. The highest is the individual who separates himself from this world for the sake of God. He does not even participate in this world, but his entire existence is concentrated on the life of the world to come. The second group is called by Abraham bar Ḥayya the 'separate community'. These busy themselves in this world but at the same time observe all the Divine commandments. They are not solitary individuals like the first group, but are a community. The third group is the 'separated nation', which like the second group is separated for the sake of heaven but has to be on guard against outsiders and therefore appoints a king to rule over them.

All these groups are separated from this world and are free of its desires. They have, for example, no lust for women and if some of these saints indulge in intercourse, it is solely for the sake of propagation. They renounce worldly possessions and are guided by the virtue of humility. Their reward is the glory and majesty of the world to come.

The question is discussed of the relative merits of the completely righteous individual—who is innately righteous and is devoid of any desire for the things of this world—and of the man who has such desires but subdues them, compelling his animal soul to be subservient to his rational soul. Although some philosophers have lauded the latter more than the former, Abraham bar Ḥayya finds the former more praiseworthy as completely fitting his ideal of a man who is free from any evil thought or inclination.

By despising this world and rejecting its preoccupations the saint draws closer to the world to come. Only one in a thousand merits this future world, namely, he whose merits exceed his faults. There is no profit to be gained from the pleasures of the world and they should only be indulged to avoid evil, e.g. one should eat to avoid the evil of hunger or wear clothes to avoid the cold. For these saints, the Divine Light is stored and their place will be close to the Divine throne, as promised in the Talmud.

This ideal of asceticism is, on the whole, exceptional in Jewish tradition. There were, of course, ascetic groups before and after Temple times and an ascetic strain can be found occasionally in the Talmud (e.g. the opinion in *Taanit* 24a, that the evil inclination can be combated by asceticism). But the general tendency in Jewish tradition is away from asceticism which is strongly opposed by Saadyal and others. Asceticism was far more typical of Christians and of certain Moslem sects, such as the Sufis, whose goal was the moral transformation of the soul through the extinction of all its passions and desires.

In medieval Jewish philosophy, the outstanding advocate of asceticism is Baḥya, who was influenced by Sufi thought. He advocates a separation from the world and its pleasures, a despising of the body and its desires so that man will be enabled to draw near to the knowledge of God. This is the same school of thought as that of Abraham bar Ḥayya and is different from the viewpoint of Judah Halevi,[1] and later of Maimonides,[2] both of whom attack excessive asceticism ('Observing the Torah is more important than abstinence', stresses Judah Halevi).

7. *Repentance*

In this life, man has free will as he has the choice between the right way and sinning; and if he sins, he still has the possibility of repentance. Sins can be committed by the heart (i.e., in the mind), by the mouth (i.e., through speaking), and through the hands (i.e., by action). A man is not liable to punishment when he sins accidentally, viz., when his heart is not in accord with his action. Neither is a man punished for what he thinks as long as the thought is not translated into action. But before a man's prayer is heard by God, he must first purify himself of all his sins.

In this context, there are five classes of men. The first two are those already mentioned in the section on the saint—the completely

[1] *Kuzari*: II, 50.   [2] *Hilkhot Deah*: III, 1, 3; Introduction to *Avot*: IV.

19

righteous and the one who all his life succeeds in subduing his evil inclinations. Then there are two types of penitent—the man who repents and does not sin again and the man who repents, but relapses into sin. And finally there is the completely wicked who never repents nor even attempts to repent. The repentance of the first two classes acquires for them life in this world and in the world to come; the repentance of the middle two types acquires only life in this world. The requirements of repentance for the sinner are that he first should cease the action and secondly cease all impure thought, and that all his actions and thoughts should be motivated only for the sake of Heaven.

The repentance of the righteous man is only for accidental deeds, while the completely righteous, who has never sinned even accidentally, is not required to repent. The way to repentance is always open but repentance or fasting are of no avail as long as one is dominated by the evil inclination. God is merciful with the wicked and gives them every opportunity to repent, but they are not forgiven entirely and punishment for their wickedness is exacted from them. When death is decreed for the wicked, it is conditional. For the wicked of non-Jewish nations repentance nullifies the decree of premature death in this world and they live out their days to the full—but as their repentance is not for the sake of God, they do not thereby acquire life in the world to come. The genuine repentance of the wicked Jew, however, when accompanied by a true reform in behaviour, acquires for him life in the world to come. For the unrepentant wicked, there is terrible suffering at the time of reckoning.

A sin committed intentionally requires confession for its expiation but not so the accidental sin which requires only repentance—and if affecting a fellow-man, a request for forgiveness. It is possible to repent of a sin after contemplating it, even though it has not actually been performed. The reward of repentance is eternal life and endless bliss.

8. *Good and evil*

Does evil originate from God? This question is posed in the last part of *The Meditation of the Sad Soul*. Biblical indications conflict.

On the one hand Jeremiah (i. 12) states: 'Then said the Lord . . . I will hasten my word to perform it' and as the word of the Lord can be for good or for evil, it would seem that He performs both good and evil. On the other hand, according to Isaiah (lv. 11) the word that issues from God is for kindness, judgment and righteousness, and from this it could be assumed that the word of God is solely to do good.

Abraham bar Ḥayya mentions that many attempts have been made to solve this problem and he cites two. The first is the theory that good is decreed absolutely and permanently whilst the evil decreed on the wicked is conditional and can be nullified in the event of their repentance. Abraham bar Ḥayya's objection is that if the latter is conditional and can be reversed by the repentance of the wicked, the former should also be issued conditionally on the righteous remaining righteous. The second theory is merely that evil is the absence of good and has no independent existence or establishment. Hence God decrees that good should be attached to a thing or be separated from it but evil itself is never directly decreed. Thus evil is not a Divine action but is absence of action, and therefore God performs only good. Abraham bar Ḥayya refutes this by quoting Isaiah lv. 7, which says specifically: 'Who maketh peace and doeth evil'.

Abraham bar Ḥayya states that God is the author of all things and their opposite—including both good and evil. These represent the Divine attribute of justice and are distributed equitably in the world. The righteous gets his fit reward, the wicked his due evil. All creations are for an appropriate purpose and evil is created for the wicked. The suffering of the righteous is only to try to test them and if they stand the test their reward will ultimately be increased accordingly. Nevertheless, Abraham bar Ḥayya also says that the completely righteous man will be saved from all trouble. Sufferings visit a person with an object—they may be as a punishment in this world for transgressions committed so that in the world to come the person who has suffered will be free from punishment. It may come to save a man from even worse straits. Similarly some wicked people prosper in this world so that they should have no excuse nor claim in the world to come. Evil, then, comes to the world to requite the wicked and to test the righteous.

On this subject of the origin of evil, Abraham bar Ḥayya prefers the religious to the philosophical solution. The theories that he rejects are those of the philosophers. The Platonists denied that evil could have a Divine origin and identified it with matter. Thus Plotinus taught that evil exists in Non-Being. As necessarily as something follows the First, so necessarily is there a last—and this last is Matter, that which has no residue of good in it. A common view among the Neo-Platonists—as among the gnostics —was that evil has no real existence. It is not-being, namely the privation and absence of good, just as darkness is the absence of light. The answer propounded by Abraham bar Ḥayya can be found in Jewish and Moslem theology. To take two examples of Moslem thought: article 6 of the *Wasiyat Abi Hanifa*, an early formulation of the Moslem creed, states 'We confess that the decision concerning good and evil depends wholly on Allah', while Al Ashari maintains that good and evil exist only by the will of God.

In Jewish tradition, the rabbis taught that God created the good and the evil inclination, while the early *Book of Creation* says 'God made one thing opposite another—and good is opposed to evil. Good is kept for good people, evil for the wicked.' Many similar examples can be adduced from the Talmud and Midrash. Among the medieval Jewish philosophers, Abraham bar Ḥayya's views are paralleled in Saadya, Baḥya and especially in Pseudo-Baḥya. Saadya, like Abraham bar Ḥayya, quotes Isaiah xlv. 7— 'Who maketh peace and createth evil'—saying that God cannot create a privation but the verse means that God creates things which can be for good or evil as man uses them.[1] Pseudo-Baḥya also discusses and rejects divergent views and concludes that God made all things and their opposites, including good and evil. This is not held by most other Jewish philosophers who find differing explanations. Thus Ibn Tzaddik says that evil is the incapacity of an object to receive good. Abraham Ibn Ezra holds that in all creation there is no evil; only good emanates from God and evil must be

[1] *Beliefs and Opinions*, p. 34.

22

traced to a defect in the object receiving the good. Ibn Daud connects evil with matter. And Maimonides states that all evils are negations and hence it cannot be said that God created evil since all His works are perfectly good. On this subject therefore Abraham bar Ḥayya is within the theological tradition, one of the few medieval Jewish philosophers to prefer this explanation to the current philosophical viewpoint.

9. The Messianic Era and the World to Come

Whatever is acquired in this world is transient and has no permanence. The important consideration is the world to come and the righteous man knows that the true life having permanence is that of the world to come. The righteous use their time in this world to establish sustenance—viz., merits accumulated by the observance of the commandments—for the world to come.

The rare person whose merits exceed his faults is rewarded with the life of the world to come. Those whose merits and faults balance should be satisfied with escaping punishment but God, in His mercy, tips the balance in their favour and grants them the world to come. In most instances, the faults exceed the merits; but God is generous to those who are 'sons of the Torah' and forgives them, although they are not thereby eligible for reward in the world to come.

By means of the Torah, Israel obtains eternal life and the reward of the world to come. Indeed all that is necessary to obtain reward in the world to come is to observe the first four commandments of the Decalogue.[1]

Man acquires the life of the world to come when he completely believes in God and His Torah. The merit of the Torah is illustrated from the period of the First Temple, when the Jews were saved despite their bad deeds, because they retained their faith in God and did not deny the principles of the Torah.

The reward of a man in this world reduces his reward in the world to come; this accounts for the prosperity of the wicked.

[1] Abraham bar Ḥayya makes an original classification of the Decalogue. After stating that the first command stands on its own, in that it comprises all the others, he divides the other nine according to two divisions: according to commands of

Suffering in this world increases reward in the world to come, hence the suffering of the righteous. If a man is oppressed and bears his burden patiently, he receives his due reward and the oppressor his due punishment in the world to come. If, however, he complains to God, God punishes the oppressor in this world but the sufferer forfeits his merit in this respect in the world to come. (Comparable are the views of Saadya who held that the wicked are rewarded in this world so that they can perish in the world to come, whereas the righteous are punished in this world so that in the world to come they will receive unmitigated reward.[1])

There is no world to come for the wicked. After death, all the souls of the wicked are commingled so that none can be distinguished from its fellow. So for the completely wicked, there is no peace either in this world or in the world to come. There is no place in the world to come for repentant non-Jews inasmuch as their repentance is not for the sake of God. So whether wicked non-Jews repent or not, their death represents complete obliteration.

In depicting the world to come to the righteous man, it is not

[1] *Beliefs and Opinions*, pp. 105-8.

thought, speech and action and according to relations between man and God, man and his family and man and man. His classification is therefore as follows:

Relations between	Man and God	Man and family	Man and man
THOUGHT	Second Command 'Thou shalt have no other God'—fear of God	Fifth Command 'Honour thy father and thy mother'	Tenth Command 'Thou shalt not covet'
SPEECH	Third Command 'Thou shalt not take the name of the Lord thy God in vain'	Sixth Command 'Thou shalt not murder' (especially one's family)	Ninth Command 'Thou shalt not bear false witness'
ACTION	Fourth Command 'Remember the Sabbath Day'	Seventh Command 'Thou shalt not commit adultery'	Eighth Command 'Thou shalt not steal'

There is the possibility of Manichean influence also on this division in that the ten commandments of the Manichees were classified as 'three with the mouth, three with the heart, three with the hand, one with the whole self'.

necessary to draw comparisons with the corporeal world. Any such comparisons made by the rabbis is for the sake of the animal soul, which has been subdued to the rational soul. The description of the life of the righteous in the world to come is familiar from rabbinic sources. In his work on geometry, Abraham bar Ḥayya describes it as 'Life without death; being without not-being'.[1] For those who have subdued their animal souls, the world to come is described in terms of this world as a place of pleasure without pain or suffering—unlike this world where pleasure is always tainted by pain.

The decrees of the world to come are not conditional and therefore there can be no repentance after death. After death there is also no free will; during his lifetime, a man knows the alternatives before him and he has the possibility to repent and choose the right path—but the dead know nothing and have no choice between right and wrong. This is why the actions of one's descendants after death can make no difference to the dead man (with the exceptions of the restoration of property that he has stolen and the teaching of Torah by his disciples, which increase his reward).

At the time of salvation, all the wicked will be destroyed and have no further existence. At this period, God will abolish all that is evil including enmity and violence while the evil inclination will not have sway over the soul any longer. All wicked people will perish as will most nations of the earth; only Israel and those of other nations who are willing to accept the Torah will survive. Israel too will be tested—but unlike other nations, a remnant will survive.

Just as man is superior to all other animals, so is Israel superior to all other nations. Israel was especially created and formed and Abraham bar Ḥayya quotes the rabbinic saying that the world was created only for Israel.[2] A person who has merit before God is not complete unless he has also merit before Israel. This superiority is not denied to the rest of mankind and the gates of repentance, i.e. acceptance of the Torah, are open to all. The Torah guarantees a long life in this world and eternal life in the world to come. After

[1] *Plane and Solid Geometry*, p. 1.   [2] *Scroll of the Revealer*, p. 3.

25

the period of salvation, those who survive—viz., Israel—will not have the power to transgress it. In his letter to Judah ben Barzillai, Abraham bar Ḥayya comments that were it not for the Torah, the world would have returned to its primeval state.[1]

All the troubles that God has brought upon Israel will be visited on the other nations at the time of salvation. Israel will be tested at that time so as to remove those who lack faith and to ensure that those who survive will be completely pure. This salvation will immediately follow the repentance of Israel in the days of their exile. It will be followed by the Resurrection of the Dead.[2] Only Israel will be resurrected—the righteous to eternal life, the sinners to eternal justice.[3] At this time, the soul, the 'breath of life' will return to its original body.[4]

THE SIGNIFICANCE OF ABRAHAM BAR ḤAYYA

Although the individual elements of Abraham bar Ḥayya's thought can generally be isolated and identified with the thought of other Jewish and non-Jewish philosophers of his period, his combination of Neo-Platonic, Aristotelian and Rabbinic thought is original as are the details of his Midrashic application and expositions. Many aspects of his philosophy consist of the Neo-Platonic theories current among Arabs and Jews in the tenth and eleventh century. But there is sufficient deviation to enable the latest writer on Abraham bar Ḥayya to call him 'the first Jewish philosopher to adopt the fundamental concepts of Aristotle'.[5] In other words, Abraham bar Ḥayya retains his individuality and cannot be comfortably pigeonholed as an appendage to the Jewish Neo-Platonists, as has been the tendency with most historians of Jewish thought. He is sufficiently independent also to reject philosophical in favour of rabbinic theories when he deems it necessary, as in his discussion of good and evil.

His writing is, for the most part, simple and clear in thought, language and style. It must be remembered that he was one of the first, perhaps even the first, to express such ideas in Hebrew—and he was writing for Jews, to many of whom such thought was

---

[1] *Letter*, p. 27.   [2] *Scroll of the Revealer*, p. 83.   [3] ibid., p. 102.   [4] ibid., p. 60.
[5] Stitskin, op. cit.

novel. It is instructive to compare the note of the author known as Pseudo-Baḥya, writing a similar type of work at about the same time—but in Arabic. He says about the exegesis of the phrase *Tohu* and *Bohu*—which he refers to matter—'I wanted to conceal the explanation of this verse and I was afraid to write it, because it was so remote from the understanding of the multitude—but I changed my mind and explained it, so that the person who can appreciate this explanation will be glad and I will have some share in his rejoicing'.[1] Pseudo-Baḥya was referring to readers in the Arabic language, for whom philosophic thought would have been no novelty. On the other hand, to Abraham bar Ḥayya's readers —many of them probably in Southern France and unacquainted with Arabic—the philosophical sections of *Meditation of the Sad Soul* and *Scroll of the Revealer* would have come as a complete innovation. Consequently, by his exegetical skill, Abraham bar Ḥayya is at pains to show at each stage that his philosophy harmonizes with the Bible and can be inferred from it. This had been the method adopted by most of the earlier Jewish philosophers such as Saadya, who explained that there is no objection to Jews speculating or writing philosophical works about the fundaments of faith as long as they based them on the Scriptures and do not rely merely on human theories as to the beginnings of the world and eternal truths. The writings of Abraham bar Ḥayya, together with his contemporary Judah ben Barzillai's commentary on the *Book of Creation*, were the first attempts to present in Hebrew what other Jewish thinkers had been writing in Arabic. They would have been particularly directed—as were Abraham bar Ḥayya's scientific works—to those Jews who did not know Arabic; which may have included some of the Jews of Catalonia as well as those in Provence.

It is clear that Abraham bar Ḥayya was widely read in Jewish and Arabic philosophy. It has been maintained that he knew, at least indirectly, the writings of Church Fathers[2] and he himself

---

[1] Pseudo-Baḥya, op. cit., p. 15.
[2] F. Baer, 'Eine jüdische Messias-prophetie auf das Jahr 1186 und der dritte Kreuzzug', *Monatsschrift für Geschichte und Wissenschaft des Judentums*. LXX (1926). Julius Guttmann in his *Philosophies of Judaism* (New York 1964), p. 114, describes

mentions that he had conversations with a monk.[1] The more Abraham bar Ḥayya is studied the more complex appear his sources and it becomes impossible to postulate any main source for his thought as was done for example by Bloch,[2] who held that he drew mainly from Baḥya, or Sarton who said that his main source was Ibn Gabirol.[3] Dubnow describes the *Meditation of the Sad Soul* as 'tiers of thought including Aristotle's *Ethics*, Plato's *Phaedo*, Gabirol and Baḥya'.[4] These generalizations are over-optimistic and unwise. Thus the debt to Aristotle's *Ethics* and Plato's *Phaedo* is negligible although there are important traces of their other writings, especially those of Aristotle whose influence, growing after the time of Alfarabi, can be frequently distinguished. Elements of his doctrine on Light and Form and Matter are held in common with Ibn Gabirol (from whom he may have drawn or both may have had a common source)—but there are also important differences. Similarly some of his ethical ideas can be found in Baḥya. A much more convincing parallel, however, is the work *Reflections of the Soul* formerly attributed to Baḥya but now assigned to another, unknown author. The date of this book, however, is uncertain. As it quotes Avicenna, it cannot be earlier than the first part of the eleventh century but its *terminus ad quem* cannot be fixed, and there is no means of fixing the order of precedence between it and the *Meditation of the Sad Soul*. Pseudo-Baḥya is more consistently Neo-Platonic than Abraham bar Ḥayya, but the object of his work is similar and both works take

[1] *Secret of Intercalation*, p. 45.
[2] *Die jüdische Literatur* (Leipzig 1892–5), edited by J. Winter and A. Wünsche, Vol. II, p. 735.
[3] G. Sarton, *Introduction to the History of Science* (Washington 1927), Vol. II, p. 206.
[4] S. Dubnow, *Die Weltgeschichte des jüdischen Volkes in Europa* (Berlin 1925–9), Vol. IV, p. 380.

Abraham bar Ḥayya's philosophy of history which is expounded in the *Scroll of the Revealer*. This is founded upon an exact correspondence between world eras and the days of creation. The division of the world into periods according to this analogy provides a pattern in which a vast number of detailed calculations and constructions can be fitted. Guttmann comments that this analogy is familiar in the historical speculations of the Church Fathers 'but this is the first instance of Christian speculation exerting a direct influence upon Jewish philosophy in the Middle Ages'.

28

considerable pains to justify their cosmogony through an interpretation of the first section of the Book of Genesis and, although
individual interpretations differ, both lie within a similar tradition.
The *Reflections of the Soul* is a more consistently philosophical work
than the *Meditation of the Sad Soul* and if written first could have
been an important source—but the uncertainty of dating makes it
impossible to postulate the relationship with any certainty.

It has been suggested that the *Meditation of the Sad Soul* contains
four homilies for the Ten Days of Penitence—the first being
delivered on the New Year; the second part on the morning of the
Day of Atonement; the third part on the afternoon of the Day of
Atonement; and the fourth part on the intermediate Sabbath. The
basis for this theory is that the second and third parts deal with
repentance and are based on a verse by verse exposition of the
prophetical readings for the morning and afternoon services on
the Day of Atonement (Isaiah lvii. 14–lviii. 14 and the Book of
Jonah). However, the other two identifications are far-fetched.
Although there is a rabbinic theory that the world was created on
the New Year, there is nothing in the first part of the book to
connect with the New Year and its mood, while there is no
apparent link between the last part and the intermediate Sabbath.
It is impossible to tell whether any parts of the book were ever
publicly delivered as sermons. In the case of the *Scroll of the
Revealer*, however, it would appear that Abraham bar Ḥayya had
made known at least his Messianic views before committing them
to writing as he mentions people who sneered at and objected to
the theories contained therein. It also appears that objections were
raised to his basing his philosophy on biblical and homiletical
proofs and it was pointed out to him that other people could
expound the same verses and reach entirely different conclusions.[1]

Abraham bar Ḥayya's Hebrew is simple and not yet encum-
bered with the complex abstruse terminology of the Tibbonides.
It is similar to the style of the late Midrashim and to the little
Hebrew that is known from contemporary Catalan documents.
The vocabulary is composed of Biblical, Talmudic and Midrashic
words together with words coined closer to Abraham bar Ḥayya's

Scroll of the Revealer, p. 74.

29

own times such as are found, for example, in Ibn Gabirol's Hebrew writings, in Judah ben Barzillai and in Gaonic responsa. Often in his scientific writings and sometimes in his philosophical works, Abraham bar Ḥayya has to coin new words to convey meanings not previously expressed in Hebrew and some of these have passed into the language. Wherever possible he bases his words on previous Hebrew usage but he is often influenced by Arabic parallels.[1] Rabin has written 'the choice of a type of Mishnaic Hebrew by Abraham bar Ḥayya must be considered the most important event in the history of the language from the cessation of spoken Hebrew until its revival in the nineteenth century'.[2]

Abraham bar Ḥayya's achievement, then, was that he developed new nuances in medieval Jewish philosophy; expounded a line of thought that was probably completely unfamiliar to most of his readers, or hearers; expressed it for them in Hebrew; described it in a clear and lucid style; and showed the compatibility of his doctrine with the Supreme Authority—the Torah.

[1] For example, the word *merkaz*, first used in the *Meditation of the Sad Soul* and explained from the Arabic, became the accepted Hebrew word for 'centre'.
[2] Chaim Rabin, 'The syntactical development of post-Biblical Hebrew' (unpublished).

The text of the *Meditation of the Sad Soul* was published by the German scholar E. Freimann in Leipzig in 1860 with a Hebrew introduction by himself and a long comment by S. J. L. Rapoport. This edition is based on a single manuscript existing in Leipzig. The text is frequently faulty and Freimann has to hazard many emendations.

The present translation has been based on a critical co-ordination of six manuscripts (together with a comparison with the lengthy citations from the first part contained in Jacob ben Sheshet of Gerondi's *Sepher Meshiv Devarim Nekhoḥim* in Bodleian MS. Op. 239). The other five manuscripts include two of the complete work, one from the Vatican (279) and the other in the British Museum (Or 832). The latter is dated in 1384 and is closely connected with the Leipzig manuscript, embodying many of its obvious errors. The best manuscript by far is the Vatican version. This not only corrects the faulty readings of the other two but embodies considerable additions which logically round off various sections; they have all been incorporated in the translation.

Three manuscripts in the Bodleian are of the first part only. They are Poc. 296 (in a Syrian hand), Seld. Superius 104 (in a Spanish hand) and Mich. 335 (in a German hand). The latter two are often summaries of the first part (and are erroneously ascribed to Abraham Ibn Ezra). The fact that these three manuscripts are of the first part only indicate that this section—dealing with cosmology—achieved particular popularity and was copied without the rest of the work.

It is also noteworthy that most of the quotations from the *Meditation of the Sad Soul* in later literature refer to this first part.

SELECTED BIBLIOGRAPHY

W. Bacher: *Die Bibelexegese der jüdischen Religionsphilosophen des Mittelalters vor Maimuni*. Strassburg 1892.

F. Baer: 'Eine jüdische Messiasprophetie auf das Jahr 1186 und der dritte Kreuzzug'. *Monatsschrift für Geschichte und Wissenschaft des Judentums*. LXX (1926)

I. Efros: *The Problem of Space in Medieval Jewish Philosophy*. New York 1917

I. Efros: 'Studies in Pre-Tibbonian Philosophical Terminology' and 'More Studies in Pre-Tibbonian Philosophical Terminology'. *Jewish Quarterly Review*. (New Series) XVII and XX (1926–7)

Jacob Guttmann: 'Die philosophischen und ethischen Anschauungen in Abraham bar Chijja's "Hegjon-ha-Nefesch" '. *Monatsschrift für Geschichte und Wissenschaft des Judentums*. XLIV (1900)

Jacob Guttmann: 'Ueber Abraham bar Chijja's "Buch der Enthüllung" '. *Monatsschrift für Geschichte und Wissenschaft des Judentums*. XLVII (1903)

M. Guttmann: 'Abraham bar Hiyya'. *Ha-Tsofe*. I (1912) (Hebrew)

I. Husik: *History of Medieval Jewish Philosophy*. Philadelphia 1942

J. Millás y Vallicrosa: *Estudios sobre historia de la ciencia española*. Barcelona 1949

J. Millás y Vallicrosa: 'La obra enciclopédica Yesode ha-Tebuna w-Migdal ha-Emuna de R. Abraham bar Hiyya Ha-Bargeloni'. *Hebrew College Annual*. XXIII (i)

J. Millás y Vallicrosa: *Nuevos estudios sobre historia de la ciencia española*. Barcelona 1960

C. Rabin: 'Abraham bar Hayya and the Revival of our Language in the Middle Ages'. *Metzuda*. III–IV (1945) (Hebrew)

J. Sarachek: *The Doctrine of the Messiah in Medieval Jewish Literature*. New York 1932

G. Sarton: *Introduction to the History of Science*. Washington 1927.

G. Scholem: 'Reste neuplatonischer Spekulation in der Mystik der deutschen Chassidim und ihre Vermittlung durch Abraham bar Chiya'. *Monatsschrift für Geschichte und Wissenschaft des Judentums*. LXXV (1931)

G. Scholem: 'A study of the theory of transmigration in Kabbalah during the thirteenth century'. *Tarbitz*. XVI (1945) (Hebrew)

M. Steinschneider: *Abraham Judaeus Savasorda und Ibn Ezra*. Leipzig 1867

Leon D. Stitskin: *Judaism as a Philosophy*. New York 1960 ,

G. Vajda: 'Abraham bar Hiyya et Al-Farabi'. *Revue des Études juives*. CIV (1938)

G. Vajda: 'Les Idées philosophiques et théologiques d'Abraham bar Hiyya'. *Archives d'histoire doctrinale et littéraire du moyen âge*. XV (1946)

G. Vajda: 'Le Système des sciences exposé par Abraham bar Hiyya et une page de Juda ben Barzillai' *Sefarad*. 1962

D. Zakkai: 'Was Abraham bar Hiyya the discoverer of double stars?' *Tarbitz*. XII (1941) (Hebrew)

B. Ziemlich: 'Abraham bar Hiyya und Jehuda Halevi'. *Monatsschrift für Geschichte und Wissenschaft des Judentums*. XXIX (1860)

WORKS OF ABRAHAM BAR ḤAYYA

The Secret of Intercalation: edited by H. Filipowski, London 1851

Plane and Solid Geometry: edited by Jacob Guttmann: Part I, Berlin 1912; Part II, Berlin 1913

The Reckoning of Astral Motions: unpublished (Oxford MS)

The Form of the Earth and the Structure of the Heavenly Orbs: edited by M. Jaffe and Jonathan ben Joseph, Offenbach 1720

The Foundations of Understanding and the Tower of Faith: unpublished

Astronomical and astrological tables: unpublished

The Scroll of the Revealer: edited by A. Poznanski, Berlin 1921

Meditation of the Sad Soul: edited by E. Friemann, Leipzig, 1860

THE MEDITATION OF THE SAD SOUL

As it knocks on the doors of repentance—and stands by its doors.
Part One. The beginning of the world and its nature.
Part Two. The good way of life in this world.
Part Three. How the sinner can be rescued from his wicked ways through contrition and repentance.
Part Four. The passing-away of man and the latter end of the world.

The beginning of the world and its nature

———————

THE MEDITATION COMMENCES with the praise of God. Rabbi
Abraham bar Ḥayya of Spain said:

Blessed is the Lord, God of Israel, Lord of every creature, great
in counsel and powerful in deeds, who teaches man wisdom, and
has granted him dominion over all that is in the world. As it is
written (Psalms viii. 7): 'Thou hast made him to have dominion
over the work of Thy hands; Thou hast put all things under his
feet'. And elsewhere (Job xxv. 6) the Bible states: 'How much
less man, that is a worm! And the son of man, that is a maggot!'
Every intelligent man should endeavour to determine what
special qualities distinguish man, who is but 'worm' and 'maggot'
and is likened to 'vanity', so that he has been granted dominion
over every creature and endowed with reason and wisdom.

We have found that most of the early non-Jewish philosophers
of discernment, who discussed religious questions—albeit without
the privilege of a knowledge of the Torah, but according to their
own wisdom and conception—have reached the conclusion that
the correct method to understand the subject properly is to
investigate the fundamentals from which all things have been
created. From the knowledge of a thing's basis and origin, its
construction can be understood. Thus, every building is composed
of its constituent stones and a person who comprehends their
arrangement will understand exactly how it is built and can

exactly reconstruct it. The Bible indicates this, when it says (Deuteronomy iv. 39): 'Know this day and lay it to thy heart, that the Lord is God in heaven above and upon the earth beneath; there is none else'. If you thoroughly comprehend the nature of the heavens above and the earth below, then you must acknowledge that God created it in its intricate structure, that He is one and there is no other God. This is the implication of the verse (Job xix. 26), 'From my flesh shall I see God', i.e., from the nature of your flesh and the structure of your organs, you can comprehend the wisdom of your Creator. This indication permits us to investigate the views of the early philosophers and their theories of creation.

These sages began by considering the form of man and demonstrated that he is the ultimate creation because he is more complex than any other creature. For the definition of man, which conveys his essence, is the 'rational animal'. 'Animal' in this definition refers to the body which grows, develops, and eventually perishes. 'Rational' refers to the power to reason logically, to differentiate between good and evil and to recognize wisdom and reason. It is wisdom and reason which distinguish man from the animals and this is conveyed in the definition by the word 'rational', the rest of the definition being common to animals.

The definition of a plant is a body which grows and eventually perishes, but does not move. This is simpler than the definition of animals, which have the power of motion, whereby they are distinguished. The definition for stones, seas, rivers, hills and valleys, etc. is that they are bodies whose forms and shapes can be changed, but they have no power to grow. Plants are therefore distinguished from them by their power of growth. The general rule is that those bodies whose form can be changed but which cannot increase in size, are the simplest of all bodies on earth. If they are compared with the heavenly bodies, the difference is that the form of the earthly bodies is changeable and temporary, whereas the form of the heavenly bodies is permanent and constant, although the term 'body' is applied in either case and the elements of the definitions are the same in both.

'Body', which is common to all created things, can be defined as width, depth and length attached to a thing that has magnitude. A careful consideration of this definition shows substance to be composed of two elements which logically are originally separate, and which existed previously in potentiality in (God's) Pure Thought until combined by His will. Ancient philosophers call one of them in Greek 'hyle' ('matter'), saying that it has no likeness or form, but is capable of receiving likeness and form. The second element they call 'Form', i.e., that which has the power to give the hyle likeness and form.

The hyle is too weak to be self-sustaining and to fill its own deficiencies, unless it is joined by the Form; while the Form cannot be perceived or sensed, unless it clothes the hyle which carries it. So each of them requires the other and is designed to enable it to exist or to be perceptible to worldly beings. Without the Form, the hyle could not exist, while the Form could not be perceived without the hyle. However, the Form is more important than the hyle, inasmuch as it only requires the hyle in order to be perceived, but it could exist on its own without being seen, whereas the hyle would not exist at all, were it not for the Form. This explains their association and relationship.

Each one of them, in turn, can be divided into two parts. The two parts of the hyle are (1) the pure, clean part; and (2) the dregs and sediment. The two parts of the Form are (1) the closed, sealed part, which is too holy to be linked with the hyle; and (2) the hollow, open section which can be attached to the hyle and be contained in it. The splendour of the self-subsistent Form, which is too pure to be linked with the hyle, spreads and shines on the hollow Form, enabling it to clothe the hyle with all forms, which the hyle is capable of receiving. These two principles, namely hyle and Form, were stored before God and existed in potentiality until such time as He saw fit to bring them out to actuality. 'Time' is used here inexactly and according to human usage, but in fact, until things went from potentiality to actuality, there was no such thing as Time, because Time existed in potentiality when all beings existed in it, for Time has no substance and is only a measure signifying the duration of existing things. Without such things, there is no duration on which Time is dependent.

They say that when [God's] Pure Thought decided to actualize them, He empowered the closed Form to come into existence and to be clothed with its splendour, without contact with the hyle. This Form, which is not connected with the hyle, is the Form of angels, seraphim, souls and all forms of the upper world. Man cannot understand or imagine such Forms, because they are not joined to something visible—and most people cannot comprehend a thing which is not perceptible by the corporeal senses. The essence of these Forms can only be grasped by the profoundly wise. These have said that this Form endured in one place with the shining light inside it. Its light spread over that Form that could combine with the hyle strengthening it—through the Word of God—to become joined to the hyle. First this Form attaches itself to the pure, clean hyle and this is a strong attachment which does not change as long as they are joined. From this union the heavenly bodies were created. Subsequently, the Form attaches itself to the impure hyle, and from this union were created all kinds of terrestrial bodies, whose forms are mutable but do not change position, such as the four elements—earth, water, air and fire—and whatever is compounded of them as far as vegetation and plants.

All their words that we have explained so far can be derived on reflection from the Torah, the Source of Wisdom. Thus the hyle and the Form, which—according to the ancient philosophers—existed in potentiality until creation, are the *Tohu* and *Bohu*,[1] mentioned in the Torah (Genesis i. 2). This was what the world consisted of, until it emerged to actuality at the word of God, as the Bible states: 'The earth was *Tohu* and *Bohu*'. If you compare the explanation of hyle given by the philosophers—viz., that which lacks shape and form and cannot exist on its own—with the meaning of *Tohu*, you will find them to be synonymous. For *Tohu* is that which has no magnitude, no sense, tangibility, or utility, as the Bible says (I Samuel xii. 21): 'After *Tohu* which cannot profit or deliver, for they are *Tohu*',[2] i.e., they have not the power to benefit themselves or others, because they are *Tohu*

[1] Translated in English versions as 'waste and void'.
[2] Translated as 'vain things'.

lacking stability, shape and form. Another verse (Isaiah xlv. 18) reads: 'He created it not *Tohu*,[1] he formed it to be inhabited' implying that *Tohu* has no stability or permanence. So that whatever they said about hyle, can be said about *Tohu*.

They described Form as that which has the power to clothe the hyle with shape and form. And the word *Bohu* is composite because it is constructed from two words—namely, *Bo* and *Hu* (i.e., 'it is' 'in it'). The Bible says '*Tohu* and *Bohu*', i.e., there is in it neither perceptibility nor permanence, or anything else in which the *Tohu* can exist. And *Bohu* is the Form which covers and sustains the *Tohu*. Proof for this can be adduced from the verse (Isaiah xxxiv. 11): 'He shall stretch over it the line of *Tohu* and the plummets of *Bohu*'.[2] The line is useless for plumbing the building, unless it sustains the plummet which shows whether the building is straight or crooked; hence the Bible connects it with *Tohu*, saying, 'the line of *Tohu*'. It connects the plummet with *Bohu*, because the plummet demonstrates whether the weight is straight or crooked, just as the Form determines the shape of what is created. The Bible says 'line of *Tohu*' in the singular, because the *Tohu*, lacking sense and permanence, is unique and has not the power to separate and divide itself. But it says 'plummets of *Bohu*' in the plural, because the covering Forms appear in many shapes.

I repeat that the word *Bohu* is composed of the two words *Bo* and *Hu*, because the clear, closed, pure Form is self-sustaining and requires no assistance, so the meaning of *Bo-Hu* is that which is self-sustaining and self-powered even though unconnected to any other thing. This explanation of *Tohu* and *Bohu* is superior to any other explanation by the philosophers.

The Bible states (Job xxvi. 7): 'He stretches out the north over *Tohu* and hangs the earth on *Belimah*'.[3] *Tohu* and *Belimah* are synonymous. This is similar to a previous verse (Job xxvi. 6) which reads: '*Sheol* is naked before Him, and *Abaddon* has no covering' where *Sheol* and *Abaddon* are synonymous, as are 'naked' and 'has no covering'. So *Tohu* and *Belimah* are identical.

[1] Generally translated as 'a waste'.
[2] Generally translated 'confusion' and 'emptiness' respectively.
[3] Generally translated as 'empty space' and 'nothing' respectively.

And because it says here: 'He stretches out the north over *Tohu*' and elsewhere (Jeremiah i. 14) it says: 'Out of the north evil shall be opened upon all the inhabitants of the land', the rabbis have said (*Baba Batra* 25b) 'The north side of the world is not enclosed', i.e., it is open and cannot sustain itself, just like the *Tohu* which cannot sustain itself. *Belimah* would then mean 'without (*beli*) Form' or 'without sustenance' because the word '*mah*' (=what?) questions a thing's essence. This can be seen from the verse (Exodus xvi. 15) 'They said to one another "What is it?" for they knew not what (*mah*) it was', i.e., they knew not what it was made for.

It can be said that the word *Mah* is the Form which is afterwards called *Mayim* (water), as it says (Genesis i. 2): 'Darkness was on the face of the deep (*Tehom*) and the spirit of God hovered over the face of the waters (*Mayim*)'. Darkness is a thing without form which was covering the *Tehom*. And *Tehom* is the same word as *Tohu*; the final letter *mem* is added as in the word *ḥinnam*, meaning a gift without a price, derived from the root *ḥanan* in Genesis xxxiii. 5: 'The children whom God hath graciously given (*ḥanan*), thy servant' or the word 'emptiness' (*reykam*) derived from 'empty' (*reyk*). In both these cases the *mem* is added, and so too *Tehom* is derived from *Tohu*.

Do not be surprised that the word *Tehom* has another meaning; most words in Hebrew—and also in other languages—are used homonymously with many meanings. Thus you find *Mayim* used for Form. *Mayim* is the plural of *Mah*, just as *shanim* is the plural of *shanah*, *seyot* is the plural of *seh*, and *piyyot* the plural of *peh* (only *mayim* has the masculine plural ending, and *seyot* and *piyyot* the feminine plural). And *Mayim* is used homonymously for Form, actual water, and other things. So the Bible calls the Form by two names—*Bohu* and *Mayim*—because one name—viz., *Bohu* —is composed of two words; one of which can be compared to *Tohu* which is sustained within it (*bo*) and the other to *Bohu* for it (*hu*) is self-sustaining, as we have already mentioned. The word *Bohu* does not therefore explain the unique aspect of Form, and another name was required to convey this aspect—namely *Mayim*.

42

The next verse explains the Pure Form which is self-subsistent and brings it out to actuality; it calls it 'light' saying (Genesis i. 3): 'Let there be light, and there was light'. This light is the Form of which the philosophers said that it has no body, nor is it connected with body. This Form does not need to be encompassed by space, but can itself serve as the space for another body; for space is that which envelops the shape of a body all around from the outside. The Bible refers to this when it says (Genesis i. 6): 'Let there be a firmament in the midst of the waters and let it divide the waters from the waters'. 'Firmament' in this context is the Form which becomes attached to the pure, clear part of the hyle, and remains inseparable from the hyle as long as it exists. It says: 'Let there be a firmament in the midst of the waters' to show that the firmament is stored in the midst of the bright light created on the first day, and that light surrounds it on all sides and serves as its space and helps it to be supported and to exist. The *Mayim* is the comprehensive Form from which all forms are derived.

When Scripture says that the firmament makes a division between the waters (*Mayim*) and the waters, it means that it makes a division between that Form which does not become attached to a body at all—namely the Light created on the first day—and that Form, which is attached to a body but which is mutable—namely all that was created on the third day. The firmament stands between them in a form attached inseparably to a body as long as it endures. This is the proper explanation of the Biblical phrase 'divides the waters from the waters' which does not refer to actual water, this being an unthinkable explanation so long as we are able to describe it philosophically without doing violence to the language.

Similarly the Bible says (Psalms cxlviii. 4): 'Praise Him, ye heavens of heavens, and ye waters that are above the heavens' meaning the Form of the clear light that is above the heavens and not referring to actual water, as has been understood by most people who are not acquainted with philosophy. If that had indeed been its intention, it would have had to mention the waters below the heavens, just as it mentions the waters above. It does not do so, but mentions the derivatives of water, namely snow and vapour (verse 8) in order to show that the waters above are not actual water, but pure, clean Form.

Do not doubt the words of our sages that before God there are stores of water to rain down on the earth and that there is water in the firmament. You must know that before Him are stocks of water, wind, snow and vapour, bread and food, silver and gold, because everything comes into being through His word; but they do not exist before Him corporeally. This is the view of all who believe in and comprehend His glory—upon whom all men should rely—and is the view of our Rabbis. If you find a saying that differs from this explanation it is only to make it clear to most of mankind who can only comprehend what they actually perceive in this world.

I return now to my main subject and say: Form is spoken of in three meanings. (1) Simple self-sustaining Form to which no body is attached, i.e., the light created on the first day. (2) Form that is joined to a body and covers it inseparably, i.e., the firmament created on the second day. (3) Form that is joined to a body as in (2) but not firmly—and it moves from form to form in two ways. Some bodies cast off one form and put on another, but cannot extend the form. Others can extend their form, but cannot cast it off. These are the creatures of the third day, which came into being at the two Divine behests. These changes occur in them all the time but none of them can alter its position. These are the forms which have been explained above according to the philosophers.

The bodies which do not change their place, are the three forms mentioned—and there are no others. (1) Body which does not change its form at all; (2) Body which can change its form, but not its dimensions; (3) Body that can change its dimension and alter its form. There is no body that can change its dimension but not its form, because by changing its dimension it alters its form, and the form of what is broad is different from the form of what is narrow, and the form of what is long is different from the form of what is short. So that it can be confidently stated that only these bodies mentioned above do not change their position.

The philosophers have said that after the body was established immutably in its place, light spread from the self-sustaining Form

44

at the Word of God. The splendour of that light spread over the body of the firmament, moving from point to point and from part to part, causing the form attached to the body to change its place. These are the bodies of the stars, which change their places, but not their form. From this spreading light which touches the firmament, the splendour extended, until it touched the body with the changing form—and from that splendour was created all three types of living things, viz., those that swim in the water, those that fly in the air, and those that move on the earth. These comprehend every type of motion possible on earth corresponding to the three elements in which living beings can exist—viz., water, air and earth (no living creature can exist in fire, *a fortiori* move in it). So there are three types of motion in the sublunar world—any other possibility can only be a combination of these and is therefore included in them. But the motion of the firmament and the heavenly bodies is different, inasmuch as it is circular and revolutionary, encircling all things beneath so as to encompass and limit them. The total types of motion are therefore four—not more, not less—and they all exist because of the light emanating a second time from the self-sustaining Form, and spreading on those forms which are attached to body, according to the philosophers. This light is the luminaries and stars created on the fourth day with the saying (Genesis i. 14) 'Let there be light in the firmament of the heaven', which the Bible subsequently divides into the two luminaries and the stars (Genesis i. 17) 'And He set them in the firmament of the heaven to give light upon the earth'. It says 'to give light upon the earth', because from that light which was placed in the firmament, God empowered the forms of bodies on earth to acquire a living spirit, and from that power were created fish, fowl, beasts and animals, i.e., those species of living things which came out to actuality by means of the water and the earth on the fifth and sixth days of creation.

The changes, which can affect a body to which Form is attached, can be divided as follows:

(1) Some of these changes affect the body externally, but these bodies do not change their form. These are the celestial creations, viz., the firmament and the stars.

(2) Others change the form (of the bodies). (*a*) Some of these touch the body but (the form) remains unchanged; (*b*) others affect the body and change their positions. These are all subsolar creations.

Now we will discuss the four categories in which Form can exist:

(1) Self-subsistent Form which never combines with matter, such as all the previously-mentioned forms in the upper world.

(2) Form that is attached firmly and inseparably to matter; and its form cannot change under any circumstances—such as the form of the firmament and the stars.

(3) Form attached to matter temporarily, but moving from body to body and changing shape, namely the bodies of terrestrial beings. These two forms, which are joined to matter, have not the power to separate from matter and exist apart from it as they had done originally.

(4) There is one more part which can logically exist, and this is form which is attached to a body, but is eventually separated from it and returns to its pristine condition to exist on its own without matter. 'Matter' here is what we originally called '*Tohu*' but now call 'creature' or 'created thing'. This remaining division is, according to the philosophers, the human soul. Reason and logic force us to admit that there exists a created form which clothes matter, and after its creation merits separation from matter becoming self-subsistent as originally. And we find no Form deserving this other than the human soul.

They have said that the human soul has health and sickness, life and death. Its sickness is ignorance, its health—wisdom. Its life is the fear of God and the performance of good deeds, which we call piety. Its death is the contempt for the glory of God and the performance of evil deeds, which we call wickedness. So it can be said that if the soul is healthy and alive, the man is called wise and pious; if healthy and dead, he is wise and wicked; if sick and living, he is ignorant and pious; if sick and dead, he is ignorant and wicked.

(1) *The wise and pious:* When he leaves the world, his soul, as a result of his wisdom, will be separated from the material world

and will resume its former form; on account of his piety, which rejected worldly ways, it will ascend from the lower to the upper world and be freed from all inferior matter. It will come into contact with the high, pure, pristine Form and enter it inseparably.

(2) *The wise and wicked:* On account of his wisdom, his soul will be freed from matter and will be self-subsistent as originally. But because of his wickedness, which inclined to worldly desires, it will not be able to liberate itself completely from worldly matter. The best it can achieve will be liberation from the transitory, i.e., subsolar, world, and it will touch the created world which does not change its form. It will move beneath the light of the sun, the strong heat of which will seem like an eternal scorching fire, but it will have neither power nor permission to emerge beyond the boundary of the firmament to reach the upper light.

(3) *The ignorant and pious:* Because of his piety in despising the world, his soul will be liberated from matter and be self-subsistent; but because of his ignorance, in not comprehending the path of wisdom or understanding the incorporeality of the soul, his soul is unable to free itself from the atmosphere of the lower world, and because it remains there, it becomes reattached to matter time and again, until it eventually acquires the wisdom by which it can liberate itself from the lower world and ascend above it. Its final station will be determined by its degree of piety or wickedness at that time.

(4) *The ignorant and wicked:* His soul is unable to extricate itself completely from matter and his death is that of an animal.

These are the views propounded by the philosophers in the light of their own understanding and reasoning. They all agree that the only way to achieve liberation from the transient, material world, in whose depths we are sunk, is through wisdom and good deeds. But these men lack the understanding to delineate the nature of the wisdom and right conduct, by which we can be liberated, because God has not granted them the privilege of receiving the holy Torah, the source of all wisdom and salvation. If they were to teach us what they mean by wisdom, we would pay no attention to them.

Consequently we go back to the subjects about which they

have spoken, but we explain them according to the Torah and in this light we can interpret their theories. We say that all things existing in this world can be divided into two categories:

(1) Those whose form is permanent; and

(2) Those whose form is changeable and hence lack permanence.

If you compare their way in this world with that in the next, you will reach four divisions:

(1) Those worthy of permanence in this world and the world to come;

(2) Those that are permanent in this world, but not in the world to come;

(3) Those that are permanent neither in this world nor in the world to come;

(4) Those that have no permanence in this world, but are permanent in the world to come.

No fifth category is conceivable. We will, therefore, examine these four categories in the creation story and through them we can learn the nature of all things.

Whatever comes into being through the Divine 'Let there be'—which was a decree calling into being and existence—has permanence in this world. Conversely, what is not described as having come into being through the Divine 'Let there be' has no permanence in this world. Let us now apply this to the four above-mentioned categories.

(1) The first Divine decree was for the creation of light (Genesis i. 3) 'And God said: Let there be light. And there was light.' Since the decree began with the words 'Let there be' that light will exist as long as the world because this decree is for the sake of creations of this world. But it immediately continues 'And there was light' to show that the Divine decree is established through it and strengthens it for the future, enabling it to exist eternally, i.e., both in this transient world and in the eternal world to come.

(2) The firmament, the luminaries and the stars also came into being with the Divine saying: 'Let there be'; for the firmament: 'Let there be a firmament in the midst of the waters' (Genesis i. 6) and for the luminaries: 'Let there be luminaries in the firmament of the heaven' (Genesis i. 14). Consequently, they will all exist as

long as this world. But because there was no further decree in their actualization, as there was in the case of the light on the first day (i.e., by the saying 'and there was light'), they will not have permanence throughout both worlds.

After each of them is actualized, the Bible says 'And it was so'. But the word 'so'[1] is to be taken metaphorically and not literally. Because they exist by virtue of the Divine 'Let it be', they maintain their pristine form as long as this world exists; but because the Divine decree was not conferred on them fully and the 'Let there be' is only metaphorical, we learn that they will not have permanence in the world to come. Proof of this can be adduced from the verse (Isaiah li. 6): 'For the heavens shall vanish away like smoke'. It says here 'they shall vanish away' and elsewhere it says 'Let there be luminaries in the firmament of the heavens', from which we see that the luminaries and stars will share the fate of the heavens. Another verse (Isaiah xiii. 10) says: 'For the stars of the heavens and their Orions shall not give their light, and the sun shall be darkened in his going forth and the moon shall not cause her light to shine'. From this verse, we can conclude that the heavens and all their stars have no permanence in the world to come, even though they will have permanence throughout the course of this world.

(3) All lower—or subcelestial—beings were only created through the Divine 'Let there be' by virtue of the benefits they confer. Thus 'Let the waters under the heaven be gathered together unto one place' (Genesis i. 9) means that He gave the water the property to be gathered up. Or 'Let the earth put forth grass, (Genesis i. 11) implies that He gave the earth the power to put forth grass and the other growths mentioned in that section. Similarly 'Let the waters swarm' (Genesis i. 20)—He gave to the waters the property of containing living things. But in these instances there is no 'Let there be' which implies coming into existence through the Divine decree. Hence all those species are merely transitory, and they have no permanent existence in this world. It says of most of them 'And it was so' after their emergence to show that they can change their shape in this world, but have

[1] Hebrew 'ken' which could be taken from *kavven* 'to establish firmly'.

49

no permanence in the world to come. There is proof of this in the verse (Isaiah li. 6) 'The earth shall fade like a garment, and they that dwell therein shall die in like manner', i.e., the earth and all that dwell therein have no permanence in the world to come.

(4) The fourth division, which has no permanence in this world but only in the world to come, is—by *a priori* demonstration—man, whose creation is distinguished by a special Divine decree and is not included in the saying 'Let the earth bring forth living beings' (which should have included man together with animals and reptiles). We have to prove this from the Biblical description of creation. We say that man has no permanence in this world, because he is not created by 'Let there be' as was the case with light, the firmament and the luminaries. But he exists in the world to come, because at the end of the account of his creation, it states (Genesis ii. 7): 'And the man became a living soul'. The word *Va-yehi* is purposely used in this context, as it was in the case of light; it is only used in the creation chapter regarding light, man, evening and morning (the last at the end of each day). Just as light, the first created thing, exists eternally, so man—the last created thing—will exist eternally; the first and last of creation last for ever.

The Bible says 'And there was (*Va-yehi*) light' to show that all aspects of light were destined for eternal existence. But with regard to man it says 'And *the* man became (*Va-yehi*)' using the definite, selective article to show that only certain definite and selected individuals merit the world to come and not all mankind.

The next consideration is to determine from which nation are derived those destined for eternal life. This subject has not been investigated by the philosophers, because they are unable to comprehend it; the answer cannot be reached by human understanding or logical reasoning, but only through the words of the Divinely inspired Torah.

In three ways the Creation narrative distinguishes man from other created beings to indicate his superiority over all earthly creatures.

(1) All living beings were created through the agency of something else, which received Divine permission to enable these living

beings to pass into actual existence. Man, on the other hand, required no intermediary to assist in any aspect of the process of his creation.

(2) Three expressions are used for the creation of living beings.

(a) *Creating:* cf. Genesis i. 21—'And God created the great sea-monsters.'

(b) *Making:* cf. Genesis i. 25—'And God made the beast of the earth after its kind.'

(c) *Forming:* cf. Genesis ii. 19—'And out of the ground the Lord formed every beast of the field.'

The 'swarming things of the waters', viz., the fish, etc., were formed by mere 'creating' and no other expression is used because of their small importance. The beasts, animals and fowls required two activities—either 'making' and 'forming' or 'creating' and 'forming'. But man, who has a soul superior to other living beings, required all three expressions used of other creatures. Initially, the Bible speaks of 'creating' ('And God created man' in Genesis i. 27). In the course of creation, it speaks of 'forming' ('The Lord God formed man'—Genesis ii. 7); while 'making' refers to the beginning and conclusion of the Divine process of creation (at the beginning God said: 'Let us make man'—Genesis i. 26) and at the conclusion—'Male and female He made them' (Genesis i. 27). Thus the creation of man incorporates all the actions which served in the creation of other living beings, and, in addition, a soul was breathed into man, as it says (Genesis ii. 7) 'And He breathed into his nostrils the breath of life'. By this man is superior to every other creation in the subsolar world. This constitutes the second differentiation.

(3) The third difference is that God granted man dominion over other created beings, as it says (Genesis i. 26) 'And let them have dominion over the fish of the sea and over the fowl of the air and over the cattle and over all the earth'. All living beings are mentioned according to the order of their creation, beginning with the fish, which were created at the beginning of the fifth day; continuing with the fowl created at the end of the same day; and then the cattle and the creations of the sixth day. It concludes 'over all the earth', meaning over everything that exists on earth. In

this way the Bible shows that man has dominion over all earthly creatures.

Just as God has distinguished man from all other living beings and granted him superiority over them, so He has distinguished one nation and sanctified it for His glory above all mankind. As the Bible says (Isaiah xliii. 7): 'Every one that is called by My name and whom I have created for My glory; I have formed Him, yea I have made Him'. As we have explained, it is man who exists after the processes of creating, forming and making, in that order. This verse shows that those men who were created, formed and made for His glory, are called by His name. To make this clear, I rearrange the verse to read 'Every one whom I have created and formed and made for My glory is called by My name'.

An examination of the Holy Scripture to identify the people called by His name shows that this can only be Israel, as it says (Isaiah xliii. 1): 'Thus saith the Lord that created thee O Jacob and He that formed thee, O Israel: fear not, for I have redeemed thee; I have called thee by My name; thou art Mine', i.e., God created them and formed them and called them by His name. Further proof is contained in another verse (Deuteronomy xxviii. 10): 'And all the peoples of the earth shall see that thou art called by the name of the Lord and they shall be afraid of thee'.

These two verses show that it is Israel which is called by His name, and it is He who has called them by His name. Thus is it written (Deuteronomy xxvi. 17) 'Thou hast avouched the Lord this day to be thy God'. How have you avouched Him? When you said (Exodus xix. 8) 'All that the Lord has spoken we will do and we will obey'. It also says (Deuteronomy xxvi. 18) 'The Lord has avouched thee this day to be a people special unto Himself'. How has He avouched you? When He said (Exodus xx. 2): 'I am the Lord, your God'. For all the praise that Israel offers the Lord, He gives them corresponding praise. Appropriate verses from the Bible show that Israel is the nation which is called holy and created for His great name. It says that God created the earth and all that is thereon and made it in His wisdom; cf. Psalms civ. 24: 'In wisdom hast Thou made them all; the earth is full of Thy creatures'. The heavens and their hosts were made at His word; cf. Psalms xxxiii. 6: 'By the word of the Lord were the heavens made and all the host of them by the breath of His mouth'. And He created and formed his people Israel—cf. Isaiah xliii. 1: 'Thus saith the Lord that created thee, O Jacob and He that formed Thee, O Israel'. And they were created and formed for the sake of His name and glory, as it says (Isaiah xliii. 7): 'Everyone that is called by My name and for My glory I have created'. This applies only to Israel, as is apparent from the verse (Deuteronomy xxviii. 10) 'All the peoples of the earth shall see that thou art called by the name of the Lord; and they shall be afraid of thee', i.e., all the peoples on the earth will fear Israel, because they will have seen—referring to the events at Mount Sinai which could be seen by all the world.

Scripture says (Isaiah xliii. 1): 'Fear not, for I have redeemed thee; I have called thee by thy name; thou art Mine'. This verse assures Israel that they will have nothing to fear at the time of redemption, that all men will fear Israel, but Israel will fear none. All men will fear Israel because of the Torah given them at Mount Sinai, as it says (Deuteronomy xxviii. 10): 'All the peoples of the earth shall see'—shall see the events at Sinai, where it was apparent to all that you were called by the holy name, i.e., the Torah was given to you, on account of which mankind will fear, as it says (ibid.): 'And they shall be afraid of thee'. Israel will fear no man, because of their belief in God and His unity and their daily reading of the *Shema*; this is why the verse says: 'I have called thee by thy name; thou art Mine', i.e., 'I called thee by thy name' when I said 'Hear O Israel'—everyone called by name is bound to listen; 'thou art Mine' you acknowledge My unity and believe in My name. Therefore I have told you not to fear, for I have redeemed you from the land of Egypt for the sake of My name and I will grant you eternal redemption. Thus Israel's great superiority—on account of which it is called by the Divine name —is its acknowledgement of the Divine unity and the acceptance of the Torah. I do not say that such superiority is not available for the rest of mankind, for that would be wrong; we must believe that the gates of repentance are open for all who seek it; as it says

(Isaiah lv. 7) 'Let him return unto the Lord and He will have mercy on him and to our God for He will abundantly pardon'. He has mercy on all who repent. So now we must investigate the nature of repentance, which leads to that mercy and this too we will prove from the Bible.

PART TWO

The good way of life in this world

SCRIPTURE STATES (Hosea xiv. 2) 'O Israel return unto the Lord, for thou hast fallen by thy iniquity' and another verse (Isaiah lvii. 14) says 'Cast ye up, cast ye up, fence the way, take up the stumbling-block out of the way of My people'. The first verse commands repentance and mentions the cause requiring its performance, namely falling into iniquity (only a person who has fallen into iniquity is liable for repentance). A person who has not sinned is guiltless before God; his prayers and fasting proclaim his merit and he does not undertake them to atone for guilt. The second verse demonstrates the manner of repentance by commanding the removal of the stumbling-block; when this obstacle is removed, the way to repentance is clear and such repentance is acceptable. The second verse, then, teaches the act of repentance and the safeguarding of the way leading to it; and as a person who does not know the way to repentance cannot repent, it follows that the explanation of the second verse should precede that of the first.

So I start by considering the second verse. The Bible says 'Cast ye up, cast ye up, fence the way'. It repeats 'cast ye up' so as to indicate the two roads, which should be cast up; one is the way of the world to come and its good paths, the other the way of this world and its wicked desires. This is as the Bible says (Deuteronomy xxx. 15) 'See, I have set before thee this day, life and good and death and evil'. Here there are two pairs: (a) life and good; 'life' is the privilege of the world to come, while 'good' is the straight and good way followed by man in this world by virtue of which he attains the life of the world to come; (*b*) death and evil; 'death' is punishment in the world to come, and 'evil' is the bad way followed by man in this world, which makes him liable for death, i.e., loss of life in both worlds. God sets these two alternatives before His people, as it says 'I have set before thee life . . . and death' and He has commanded to choose the good way, as it says (Deuteronomy xxx. 19): 'Choose life that both thou and thy seed may live'. Since God has taught them to choose life, it follows that He has warned them to despise and keep far from the path leading to death. That is why this verse says 'cast ye up, cast ye up'—make two highways, one the good highway of the righteous, the other the bad highway of the wicked.

It says 'fence the way', i.e., put fences and borders along each of these ways, so that there will be a clear differentiation between them: make life the border of the good way and put death as the border of the bad way, so that a man should go along the right path surrounded by life on every side. It continues 'Take up the stumbling-block out of the way of My people', i.e., remove any obstacle from the path of the righteous, who are My people. It does not warn the wicked nor is apprehensive over their direction, as in the other verse, which commanded 'choose life', and it is not obliged to mention anything else.

So this verse is divided into three subjects. The first is the number of paths ('cast ye up, cast ye up'); the second, their boundaries ('fence the way'); and the third, putting the path in order and the removal of obstacles ('take up the stumbling-block').

Each of these aspects is taken up again in the next verse (Isaiah lvii. 15): 'For thus saith the high and lofty One, who dwelleth for ever, whose name is Holy; I dwell in the high and holy place with him also that is of a contrite and humble spirit, to revive the spirit of the humble and to revive the heart of the contrite ones'. This verse explains the previous one, as though asking 'Why does it repeat "cast ye up"?' and answering 'for thus saith the high and lofty One'; and because the high and lofty One has said so-and-so, the verse commands, 'cast ye up, cast ye up' (the word 'For' at the beginning of the second quotation links the two verses together).

A thorough investigation of this verse shows that it expounds the righteousness of God and His manifold mercies to mankind. God gave all His creatures—from the largest to the smallest—whatever faculties they required. He gave plants and vegetables the faculty to absorb the moisture of the water, which is connected with the very earth with which they are in contact, so as to acquire the beneficial moisture and turn it into food to nourish their bodies. He enabled that faculty to make ripe the moisture which it absorbs, so as to return it to the natural structure of the absorbing body, until it increases its shoots and produces fruit, which will perpetuate its species. To animals He gave the faculty to meet their requirements in this world and taught them to seek their food, to maintain their bodies with it, and to produce offspring, which survives them in this world. He designed their bodies according to their respective needs. He provided the carnivorous with sharp claws and teeth and great strength; the herbivorous, with lowly strength and humble spirit; birds received pinions and wings by which they could ascend and fly; while to whatever is weak and timorous, He gave swift legs, so that they could flee. Many of them fulfil their functions properly. Others fail in many respects and harm themselves, but God does not punish them or accuse them. And God created man in His image and perfected him and provided for all his requirements in this world.

There are men who fulfil all their functions as required and there are those who fall short. If human judgment on this subject resembled that of other animals, the righteous would not receive merit for his righteousness, because all he did would be predestined, while the wicked would not be punished for his evil, as his wickedness and aimlessness in this world would be sufficient. But God in His mercy has extended His goodness and grace over mankind by giving them merit for their good deeds and punishing them for their evil ways—a privilege He has not granted other living things. Man is worthy of this, because God has granted him dominion over all livings things, as it says (Genesis i. 28) 'And have dominion over the fish of the sea, over the fowl of the air and over every living thing that creepeth upon the face of the earth', obligating man to guide them and seek their welfare—this was the condition on which he was granted dominion over them. If he fulfils this condition, God increases his superiority, but if not, punishes him and diminishes his distinction.

The Bible hints at this when it says: 'For thus saith the high and lofty One'. The two words refer to the same thing—the high is lofty and the lofty is high. The difference is that 'high' (Hebrew '*ram*') can be understood absolutely as a pure Divine attribute, attributed to God's glory—height being ascribed only to God. On the other hand, 'lofty' (Hebrew '*nisa*') is a relative term, meaning loftier than something else; it is one of God's attributes in that when His glory and majesty are compared to His creatures, He is lofty and exalted above all of them. It says 'the high and lofty One', because height and loftiness are His alone, and if anything else becomes lofty, it cannot approach His height, and whatever its height, He is loftier. The two expressions, therefore, refer to the same thing.

These are followed by two other expressions, which also refer to the same thing, namely 'who dwelleth for ever whose name is holy'. 'Dwelleth' here is not like dwelling on earth, or in a house, as in 'to make His name dwell there' (Deuteronomy xiv. 23), nor does it mean finishing an action and resting after its completion, as in 'My soul had dwelt in silence' (Psalms xciv. 17) which is far from applicable to God. The meaning of 'who dwelleth' here means that He is not affected by movement or change. Because the word 'dwelleth' can mean various things in different contexts, such as living in a house, as we previously mentioned, Scripture here connects it with the word 'holy' and says 'who dwelleth for ever, whose name is holy'. Dwelling connected with holiness is applied only to God, who is immutable and unique. 'Who dwelleth for ever' means to all eternity, in an uniqueness which is too sanctified to be paralleled.

Scripture is obliged to ascribe the above-mentioned attributes to God, because it is talking about worldly characteristics, which are dependent on these attributes. First it mentions His pure attributes and then His kindnesses and favours which He bestows on mankind by virtue of these attributes. It is the way of God that when He mentions one of His attributes, He brings to the world something connected with that attribute, as the Bible says (Exodus

xx. 24): 'In every place where I mention My name I will come unto thee and I will bless thee', i.e., I bring you my blessing according to the subject I mention. This is a proof that man should make a blessing and praise God for all that he receives. And so in order to explain the great superiority which He has bestowed upon His people, it mentions the Holy names which attest to that superiority, namely 'high and lofty, who dwelleth for ever, whose name is holy'. These are the names by which He is called in the heavens, and therefore it connects them with His word as it says 'thus saith the high and lofty One, who dwelleth for ever whose name is holy', and afterwards it connects them with His kindnesses towards those who live on earth. And it says 'I dwell in the high and holy place with him also that is of a contrite and humble spirit'. He dwells in the high and holy places, but at the same time He is with the contrite and humble of this world 'to revive the spirit of the humble and to revive the heart of the contrite ones'.

These two names refer to categories of the perfectly righteous in this world. The first of them is of humble spirit and lowly soul and has no desire for any of the pleasures of this world, all his thoughts being directed to the world to come. The second desires the pleasures of this world, but conquers this desire and rejects all the good things of this world for the sake of the world to come. Of the first, it is said 'to revive the spirit of the humble', i.e., his animal soul (the 'spirit of life' which man has in common with animals) is humbled and subservient to the rational soul (the 'breath of life') and eschews all the preoccupations of this world. Referring to the second category, it says 'and to revive the heart of the contrite ones', for their heart is contrite and subdues the desire for the pleasures of this world, compelling it to be subservient to the rational soul.

The sages differ as to which of these two categories is the more praiseworthy. Many have expressed the opinion that the one who desires the pleasures of this world but subdues that desire, is more meritorious than the one who has no such longing—because the former suffers, while the latter is tranquil and at ease with himself; and the one who is pained should be regarded more highly, proportionately to the extent of his sufferings. They compare this with the cases of a young man and an old man, who both refrain from the same transgression—but the old man refrains out of the absence of desire, whereas the youth conquers his inclination. Everyone praises the youth for restraining his desires, whereas no one praises the old man who had no desire to subdue. The same would apply in the case of two young men, where one conquers his inclination, while the other does not have to; most people would praise the contrite one who subdues himself.

However, those who have examined the matter more closely contend the opposite and praise more the man whose inclination was subdued from the very outset; he is the one called 'humble of spirit'. They say that the person who first desires and then conquers his inclination, is not free from impure thoughts—but the other type never has any such thoughts. They cite the contrast between the perfectly righteous and the completely repentant man; each is praiseworthy and meritorious, but the perfectly righteous more so, because he is completely worthy, whereas the other is only worthy after the forgiveness of his sins.

There are those who think that the verse under discussion indicates that the two categories are equal, because it says first 'I dwell in the high and holy place with him also that is of a contrite and humble spirit' giving 'contrite' (the one who subdues his inclination) precedence over 'humble of spirit' (the one whose desire is automatically conquered). After that, it says 'To revive the spirit of the humble and to revive the heart of the contrite ones', here giving precedence to the humble over the contrite. It would follow then that the two categories are equal, as the first is given precedence in one instance and the second in the other. However, reflection on the subject shows that the contrite are mentioned first in the former quotation because God is contrasting His own greatness with the farthest place on earth to which His many mercies reach, and that is the deepest of the deep, and He calls that place 'depressed' (=contrite) which is lower than 'plain' (=humble). But when (in the second quotation) He grades the merit of those who fear Him—for whose sake He was contemplating this world—He mentions first the 'humble' whose soul is

60

free of any evil and who immediately ascends; only subsequently is it the turn of the 'contrite' who has been subject to impure thoughts and must purify himself of them before he is called 'righteous'. It mentions the 'spirit' of the humble, because the spirit accompanies the soul, as it says 'the breath of the spirit of life' (Genesis vii. 22); whereas in the case of the contrite it mentions the 'heart' which accompanies the body because it is the heart that is concerned for the body's desires. But we do not need to go further into this distinction.

Scripture now continues (Isaiah lvii. 16) 'For I will not contend for ever neither will I be always wroth; for the spirit should wrap from before me and the souls which I have made'. The verb 'contend' (Hebrew 'riv') in most contexts implies an argument between two men, e.g., 'If there be a contention between two men' (Deuteronomy xxv. 1) or 'The herdsmen of Gerar contended with the herdsmen of Isaac' (Genesis xxvi. 20). But in our context it means 'proof' and 'claim' as in 'Hear now my reasonings and hearken to the claim of my lips' (Job xiii. 6). So in our verse, the word 'riv' means 'proof' or 'claim', i.e., I do not claim that men should give me a reason for which they deserve reward and I do not object to their doing things merely for their own success; although they gain no merit from such action, I do not hold this against them.

It says 'Neither will I be always wroth'. I will not be wroth with the wicked who forfeit the world, by concealing from them the path to repentance, but I open the gates of repentance for them. Hence the saying (Genesis vi. 3) 'My spirit shall not strive (Heb. *yadun*) with men for ever' (taking *yadun* from the root meaning 'strive'). They say in the case of the generations before the Flood, that when they were humble of spirit and conducted themselves properly, God prolonged their years in this world, but they did not acquire merit for the world to come, because their behaviour did not have such an objective, which was unknown to them. Similarly their wicked died in the prime of life and so were punished; as it says 'My spirit shall not strive with man'—He did not require proof from them that they deserved reward or punishment in the world to come. This was the rule from generation to generation until Abraham understood the path of the fear of heaven and was worthy of the world to come. That is what the Bible means when it says 'For I will not contend for ever, neither will I be always wroth'. I will not contend with those who find the right way neither will I be wroth with those who lose it. 'For the spirit should wrap from before me and the souls which I have made.' It says 'spirit' in the singular referring to the vital soul which is in animals and all living beings whose conduct is not judged as being meritorious or otherwise; 'souls' is in the plural, referring to the soul of man which can be meritorious or guilty— and can be divided into various categories.

To explain this subject, I say that God gave man three faculties (some call them souls). The first is the faculty whereby he grows, as does vegetation. The second enables him to move. These two faculties are shared with all other animals and they are called 'breath of life'. The third faculty is the ability to distinguish between good and evil, between truth and falsehood, between everything and its contrary, and to discern wisdom. This is the soul (Heb. 'neshamah') by which man is distinguished from other animals. If this soul prevails over the animal soul, man will be distinct from animals and will be perfect and worthy. But if the animal soul prevails over the rational soul, that man is regarded as an animal and called iniquitous and wicked. The extent by which the one prevails over the other can be graded into various divisions, and that is why the plural is used.

It says 'For the spirit should wrap from before me'—the vital soul wraps all living things like an outer garment. It goes out 'from before Me' and by My permission it exists in the world. The spirit (neshamah) is superior in another respect in that I have made it and breathed it into his nostrils and for its sake I have mercy upon him and prepare the way for his salvation. This indicates the Torah, which He brought down to the world for the benefit of all who believe in it.

After this verse has expounded the fate of the completely righteous, for whose sake the Torah was brought down, it explains the fate of the wicked. It divides them into categories in each of which the animal soul prevails during their childhood, and there is a conflict between it and the rational soul, and so in the time of their maturity and old age three divisions can be distinguished:

(1) If both the rational and the animal souls are equally strong, the man will be of the average type, which is that of most individuals;

(2) If the rational soul eventually dominates, he will be in the best of the three categories;

(3) If the rational soul is totally subdued by the animal soul, he will be in the most wicked category.

Scripture begins by saying (Isaiah lvii. 17) 'For the iniquity of his covetousness was I wroth and smote him; Conceal and I was wroth and he went on turning away in the way of his heart.' The wicked man, to whom this refers, forsakes the path of truth and the service of God because of his covetousness and his appetite for the joys of this world. God is angry with him and punishes him, as it says 'I was wroth and smote him'. He then repents nominally, but his heart still harbours wickedness and stubbornness; like most hypocrites, he thinks he is deceiving God—he believes that God is not aware of this. About them the Bible says (Jeremiah ix. 8): 'One speaketh peaceably to his neighbour, but in his heart he layeth in wait for him', and the more they conceal from God in their wickedness, the more angry He is with them, as it says 'Conceal, and I was wroth', i.e., they conceal, but God in His wrath exposes them. It says 'He went on turning away in the way of his heart', referring to the wicked who continually return to their wicked ways, as it says (*Mishnah Yoma* viii. 9): 'The one who says "I will sin and afterwards I will repent", is not given the opportunity to repent'. This is the first category.

Concerning the second category, it says (Isaiah lvii. 18): 'I have seen his ways and will heal him; I will also lead him and restore comforts unto him and to his mourners'. This is the man whose rational soul struggles to the utmost with the animal soul and eventually secures the upper hand; God knows what is in his heart and understands his devotion and helps him, giving him the necessary strength, as it says 'I have seen his ways and will heal him and will lead him', for He leads him along the right path. 'And restore comforts unto him'; these comforts are the reward he receives in exchange for the desire he has subdued. This is the reward of the rational soul. 'To his mourners' is the merit for the animal soul which is desolate because it has not achieved its desire. The meaning of 'his mourners' is similar to 'shall the land mourn' (Hosea iv. 3), where the word 'to mourn' means 'to be desolate'.

It is thus apparent that the wise rational soul has no pleasure in this world, but is angry and bitter at its imprisonment; God comforts it and gives it the privilege of the world to come in recompense for its anger and bitterness. It is the animal soul that longs for the desires of this world, and it mourns and is desolate if it is denied pleasure from them; so if it is subservient to the rational soul and subdues its desire, God comforts its mourning and rewards it. So God rewards the animal soul for the merit of the rational soul, because it obeys it; and He punishes the rational soul for the guilt of the animal soul, when it has not subdued the animal soul.

It must be understood that any comparison drawn by the rabbis between this world and the merit of the world to come is only for the sake of the animal soul which is subservient to the rational soul, as its desires are rooted in this world and it has forsaken them for the glory of the rational soul. But the completely righteous man whose animal soul is under complete control and who is liberated from this-worldly desires, has a reward which requires no comparison with this world, and he dwells beneath the Divine throne with his crown on his head and enjoys the splendour of the Divine presence (cf. Tractate *Berakhot* 17a). Hence it says (Isaiah lvii. 19): 'I create the flow of the lips; Peace, peace to him that is far off and to him that is near, saith the Lord; and I will heal him'. It begins with the 'flow of the lips', the most distinctive attribute distinguishing man from animal and fowl, which make audible, but meaningless sounds; the human voice alone has 'flow', and 'fruit', cf. 'A man shall be satisfied with good by the fruit of his mouth and the recompense of a man's hands shall be rendered unto him' (Proverbs xii. 14). 'Fruit of his mouth' can only mean the speech which distinguishes him from animals and which, by proper usage, can earn him the world to come. For the Bible says he will be satisfied with good in this world and will

64

be rewarded in the world to come. It says (Proverbs xiii. 3): 'He that keepeth his mouth, keepeth his life; but he that openeth wide his lips will have destruction'. Just as his mouth can bring him benefit and preserve his soul, so it can also lead to his destruction. It says (Proverbs x. 31): 'The mouth of the just bringeth forth wisdom'; man has superiority by virtue of what his mouth says, and by proper care he is saved from evil. As already stated, when any mention is made of God's kindnesses to His servants, He is designated by the appropriate attribute; and so here, where the verse relates the reward in the world to come of the fruit of proper speech God is referred to as the 'Creator of the fruit of the lips'.

The verse continues by mentioning the benefit to be derived from 'the fruit of the lips', namely 'Peace, peace to him that is far off and to him that is near', i.e., twofold peace to the one who keeps far from the pleasures of this world; one for the world to come, which he has loved and chosen, and the second for this world that he has rejected. He will have the privilege of being surrounded by peace on all sides and this will bear no resemblance to anything in this world.

Next, it mentions the privileges granted to 'him that is near'—who inclines towards the affairs of this world, and it says 'to him that is near saith the Lord; and I will heal him'; i.e., after he approaches the sins of this world and lusts for them, but forces himself to reject them, he will be granted peace, says the Lord, who also grants him healing in place of the lust which he has rejected for God's sake. This healing will be that, in place of his this-worldly desires, he is shown beautiful likenesses and boundless pleasure in the world to come, where there is no pain and no suffering. The pleasures of this world are material and connected with suffering and sickness, whereas the good things shown by God to the righteous in the world to come are unsullied, e.g., costly pearls, and the forms of golden candlesticks and tables of gold and silver, filled with good things and dainties, as mentioned in the writings of the early rabbis, and will be shown to the righteous, who suppress their desires for the pleasures of this world. But the perfectly righteous, whose entire pleasure is the fear of heaven and the service of God, do not need to conceive the world to come in this-worldly likenesses. Concerning their merit, it says (Psalms xxxi. 20): 'How great is Thy goodness which Thou hast laid up for them that fear Thee', and also (Isaiah lxiv. 3): 'Neither has the eye seen a God beside Thee, Who worketh for him that waiteth for Him'.

After concluding the description of the reward of the righteous in the world to come, mention is made of the punishment of the wicked. It says (Isaiah lvii. 20) 'But the wicked are like the troubled sea, when it cannot rest, whose waters cast up mire and dirt'. Just as in a storm the waters of the sea are fierce and troubled and cannot be clearly discerned, so the souls of the wicked are inter-mingled and sunk in the loathsome depths of the world and are indistinguishable in this world—and their fate will be evil in the world to come.

This chapter concludes by stating that they will know no good all their days, saying (Isaiah lvii. 21): 'There is no peace, saith my God, for the wicked'. It decrees that they will have no peace, neither in this world nor in the world to come. It does not men-tion the Divine name absolutely in this verse to show that He is not their God and does not watch over them, but it says 'My God', associating Him with His people and with those who fear Him. The verse states that the righteous man says, 'My God, who grants me peace, decrees that the wicked will have no peace', as it says (Proverbs xvi. 4): 'The Lord hath made all things for Himself; yea even the wicked for the day of evil', i.e., all that God has created has an appropriate purpose, and evil was established for the wicked man—although the Lord gives him the choice between good and evil, life and death.

This section shows the two paths and their boundaries. The one path is the way of the righteous with its abundance of peace, the other, the way of the wicked from which peace is absent. Hence the verse 'Cast ye up, cast ye up, prepare the way', which also says 'Take up the stumbling-block out of the way of my people', the opening verses having shown how the stumbling-block was set up. It goes on (Isaiah lviii. 1): 'Cry aloud, spare not, lift up thy voice like a trumpet and show my people their transgression and the house of Jacob their sins'. It commands you to raise your voice without respect for persons, great or small, and not to reject His reproof, as it says 'Cry aloud, spare not, lift up thy voice'—do not refrain from telling My people their iniquities.

From this you learn two important rules about how to deliver reproofs: (1) The first rule is that you must only reprove a man who is to some extent God-fearing and worthy of God's people, as it says, 'Show My people their transgression and the house of Jacob their sins'; you do not have to reprove a person who is not of My people. As the Torah says (Leviticus xix. 17): 'Thou shalt rebuke thy fellow citizen'. This is also what it says (Proverbs ix. 7): 'If one reproveth a scorner, he getteth to himself shame; and he that rebuketh a wicked man getteth to himself his blot'. This verse warns you not to reprove the scorners and the wicked. The scorners are the opposite of the wise, as it says (Proverbs xiv. 6) 'A scorner seeketh wisdom, but findeth it not', i.e., he is under the impression that he is seeking wisdom, but he is not really fit to do so. The scorner is the opposite of the wise man, according to all (except himself—because the scorner generally regards himself as wise and knowledgeable) and because of his obstinacy he pays no attention to the one who reproves him, but maintains his evil ways. Thus when it says (Proverbs ix. 7) 'If one reproveth a scorner, he getteth to himself shame'; 'to himself' refers to the scorner, who gets disgrace on himself because he does not accept the words of correction. If you say that 'to himself' refers to the one who reproves, the meaning will be that a person who reproves a scorner brings disgrace on himself. In either instance, you must not reprove a scorner, who will not listen to you, as this will bring disgrace either on him or on you. The wicked is different in that he knows he is committing evil and persists in it. Thus it says: 'And he who rebuketh a wicked man for his blot'—you point out to him the blot of which he is already aware but he still takes no notice. This verse shows that there is no use rebuking either the scorner or the wicked, while the next verse shows what you get by rebuking them. It says (Proverbs ix. 8) 'Reprove not a scorner lest he hate thee; rebuke a wise man and he will love thee'. Do not reprove a scorner—who is the opposite of the wise—for he will hate thee, but reprove a wise man—i.e., all the God-fearing and not necessarily only those that have wisdom—and he will love thee. From this it is obvious whom you should reprove and whom you should refrain from rebuking.

(2) The second rule deals with what requires rebuke and who should be reproved. This can be deduced from the verse (Isaiah lviii.1): 'Show My people their transgression and the house of Jacob their sins'. 'Transgression' refers to speech, and 'sins' to deeds. 'My people' are the God-fearing who deserve to be called by His name and 'house of Jacob' is the rest of Israel. It follows from this, that all men, even the God-fearing and perfect, should be warned in the case of errors committed inadvertently through speech. But no wrong should be ascribed to a righteous man through his deeds, even if you see him committing a sin, because he immediately corrects himself and is grieved. As the rabbis have said (*Berakhot* 19a): 'If you see a scholar committing a transgression by night, do not harbour ill thoughts about him by day—perhaps he has repented', i.e., he has repented of his own accord and you must not embarrass him. But the rest of the house of Jacob should be warned, concerning anything of which you suspect them; as it says: 'And the house of Jacob their sins' in the plural, i.e., on any matter; 'My people, their transgression' in the singular, i.e., in this one instance.

The guilt of mankind before God derives from iniquities, transgressions and sins. The iniquities are the rebellion of the heart, the transgressions the error of the mouth, and the sins disgraceful actions. The verse explains the nature of the transgressions and the sins, but not of the iniquities, which are the rebellion of the heart and are the most serious of all, causing Divine anger, as it says (Isaiah lvii. 17): 'For the iniquity of his covetousness was I wroth and smote him.' The iniquity causes the wrath and the smiting, and that is the stumbling-block, as it says (Hosea xiv. 2): 'For thou hast fallen by thine iniquity'. And if he intends to remove the stumbling-block, as it says 'Take up the stumbling-block out of the way of My people', he has to warn specifically against the iniquity—which is the stumbling-block—together with the prohibited transgressions and sins. We can also say that man is unlike

God in that God knows the secrets of the heart but does not punish a man for his evil thoughts as long as these thoughts are not translated into speech or action; and if a man errs by speech or deeds without any inner intention, he is not punished by God. So the iniquity causes the punishment and it is the stumbling-block before God, when it is translated into speech or action. But men see the action without being aware of the motivation of the heart, as it says (I Samuel xvi. 7): 'For man looketh on outward appearance, but the Lord looketh on the heart'. When a man sees an action, he presumes that it is in accordance with the heart—and so he must, according to what appears obvious to him, issue a rebuke without examining the heart—in accordance with the saying 'Take up the stumbling-block'. So it is wrong to suspect a man who is far from suspicion, or to shame a man who will be ashamed himself. So we have covered the three subjects mentioned in the first verse: viz., the highways, the boundaries, and the removal of the stumbling-block.

The next verse explains man's conduct in worshipping God, saying (Isaiah lviii. 2) 'And Me they seek daily and desire to know My ways as a nation that did righteousness and forsook not the ordinance of their God; they ask of Me the ordinance of justice; they take delight in approaching God'. All Israel believes in the Torah and wants to follow its path, but most go astray for one of two reasons: either because the evil inclination gets the better of them or because of ignorance. The former require reproof, the latter enlightenment.

This is explained by the verse when it says 'And Me they seek daily and desire to know My ways'. 'And Me' connects this verse with the preceding one, in which I (i.e., God) commanded you to relate to them their transgression and sin; some of them seek Me but do not find the way—as it says 'And Me they seek daily', while others wish to, but do not succeed, because their evil inclination predominates, as it says 'And desire to know My ways'. The one who does not know the way is under the impression that he is following the right path 'as a nation that did righteousness' while the one whose evil inclination gets the better of him thinks that he is not acting iniquitously and that he 'forsook not the

69

ordinance of their God' and they—according to what they believe in their hearts—'ask of Me the ordinance of justice; they take delight in approaching God' but because of their mistaken view, they act wickedly before God.

It continues (Isaiah lviii. 3) 'Wherefore have we fasted and Thou seest not? Wherefore have we afflicted our soul and Thou takest no knowledge?' They appear discontented with God for not hearkening to them. He reproves them, saying 'Had you been serving me and fasting properly, you would have been heard, your needs would have been met and your guilty deeds forgiven'. As it says 'Behold in the day of your fast ye find pleasure and exact all your labours'.

After this, he rebukes each of them appropriately, starting with the category who are ruled by their evil inclination, are impudent, and complain that God does not listen to them. It says of them (Isaiah lviii. 4): 'Behold ye fast for strife and debate and to smite with the fist of wickedness; ye shall not fast as you do this day to make your voice to be heard on high'. In so far as the evil inclination rules them, it prevents them from directing their thoughts properly on their fast-days, because of the evil thoughts it provokes. As for those who endeavour to subdue their inclination but have difficulty in conquering it, if their faith is sufficiently strong, they subdue it and are rescued from their iniquity—and the forgiveness of their wickedness is their ultimate reward. But if they are not sufficiently strong to overcome their iniquity, their fasting will serve only as a reminder of their iniquity. Nobody who is dominated by his evil inclination deserves to have his fast accepted, unless he repents of his evil ways; as it says 'Ye shall not fast as ye do this day, to make your voice to be heard on high', i.e., if that is the nature of your fast, your voice will not be heard. This is the rebuke to the sinner who is dominated by his evil inclination but yet appears at Divine service, and to all such haughty hypocrites. It asks those who are insincere (Isaiah lviii. 5): 'Is such the fast that I have chosen? A day for a man to afflict his soul? Is it to bow his head like a bulrush and to spread sackcloth and ashes under him? Wilt thou call that a fast and an acceptable day to the Lord?' The fast that God desires is not that a man humble himself, cast down his eyes, spread dust and ashes beneath him and appear to be mourning and grieving, while God knows that he is a deceiver and liar and that, while he restrains his mouth from food and drink, he is not restraining his heart and tongue from evil meditation. An act of affliction is not called 'fast' or 'an acceptable day to the Lord'. The proper form of fast is indicated in the next verse (Isaiah lviii. 6): 'Is not this the fast that I have chosen? To loose the bands of wickedness, to undo the heavy burdens, to let the oppressed go free and that ye break every yoke?' It speaks here about the man who is overcome by the evil inclination, and is subdued by it at the time of the fast, and it does not let him direct his heart. This is the person meant when it says 'Behold ye fast for strife and debate', and they are the ones of whom it says: 'They say "I sin and afterwards I will repent", but God does not give them the opportunity to repent'. Similarly, God is angry with those who say 'I sin and the Day of Atonement will make the repentance'.[1]

In every instance where they err, Scripture postulates an alternative by which they could acquire merit if they were to act properly. Instead of 'to smite with the fist of wickedness' stated above, it says here 'to loose the bands of wickedness', i.e., your fast is not acceptable as long as you think wickedly 'and smite with the fist of wickedness' but if you loosen the bands of wickedness, namely stubbornness and evil thoughts, you will be worthy to hear and to receive. And instead of what is said above—'Behold ye fast for strife and debate', it here commands that one should keep far from strife and evil, saying 'Undo the heavy burdens'. It says 'that ye break every yoke', meaning that you should bring peace between two quarrelling men who are banded together to go astray and to quarrel. 'That ye break every yoke', i.e., that you should break from your heart all thoughts of vengeance concerning your fellow-men, which is a departure from the proper way.

It says 'Let the oppressed go free' referring to the souls of those men who are the prisoners of their evil inclinations; you must release them from this servitude. Then all the yokes of the wicked will be broken and the souls enmeshed in the power of the evil

[1] cf. *Mishnah Yoma*: VIII, 9 and B. *Yoma*: 85b.

inclination will be saved. The next verse (Isaiah lviii. 7) continues: 'Is it not to deal thy bread to the hungry and that thou bring the poor that are cast out to thy house? When thou seest the naked that thou cover him; and that thou hide not thyself from thine own flesh?' This shows the path of humility and righteousness to all who seek it, but do not know where to find it. In place of what it said previously (in verse 5) 'A day for a man to afflict his soul', it now says 'Is it not to deal thy bread to the hungry?', i.e., if you afflict your souls and starve yourselves, this will not be accounted righteousness until you have fed the hungry. And in place of what it said 'Is it to bow down his head as a bulrush?', it now says 'That thou bring the poor that are cast out to thy house', i.e., worship and fear of God do not consist in bowing your heads and putting on an expression of pain, but in bringing the poor and the downcast to your house, and in removing their troubles in so far as it lies in your power. And in place of 'And spread sackcloth and ashes', it says, 'When thou seest the naked, that thou cover him', i.e., do not think that you will receive a reward merely for wearing sackcloth and spreading ashes under you, whereas at the same time you refuse the opportunity to clothe one of your naked fellow-men, or abstain from assisting some lowly and weak individual.

The verse concludes 'That thou hide not thyself from thine own flesh'. Most commentators deduce from this that a man is more obliged to perform kindnesses for his own kith and kin, than for other people—and this is obvious from many quotations. A further meaning here is to take 'thine own flesh' as your factual body and that you should not hide yourself from it, i.e., not starve it too much. As you are commanded to feed the hungry man, it follows that you must not starve yourself or weaken your body; God has not ordered you to starve but only to afflict yourself, as it says (Numbers xix. 7): 'Ye shall afflict your souls'.

Afflicting the soul involves withholding it from all evil thoughts and desires of this world, so that it will separate itself from all carnal actions and all the desirable things of this world and will contemplate the holiness and wonders of the upper world. But as not every man's soul is properly subdued as long as it is not

72

afflicted, we are commanded to afflict and starve the body on the day that the soul is afflicted (viz., the Day of Atonement). The original intention is the affliction of the soul and from this derives the need to afflict and starve the body. There is proof for this in that you are permitted to feed the sick and weak (on a fast-day) if you fear for him, but you are not permitted to relax the affliction of his soul—rather should he die a hundred times than commit a transgression. So the main thing is the affliction of the soul. It can be that he who afflicts his soul on days other than those when he is commanded to afflict himself (i.e., by afflicting his mouth in eschewing all vain and idle words and speaking only words of wisdom and Torah, and afflicting his heart so as not to think evil or consider the affairs of this world but direct it to concentrate on the might and wonders of God)—that this will be accounted to him as fasting and affliction all his life even if he does not refrain from permitted foods and drink. However, if he starves his body but does not afflict his soul, the sages say that he will be punished for the hunger of his soul and receive no reward for his body's fasting.

You see in this world men who want to go in the right way and afflict their body and frequently abstain from food and drink, yet they fail to afflict their souls. Even as they fast, they are busy with this-worldly affairs according to their own convenience and indulge in idle talk and in matters which can lead to obscenity. According to all the sages, such men are observing matters of secondary importance, but neglecting the main thing. The proper form of affliction before God is to keep far from all pollutions of mouth and body, ensuring that the body should have no domination so that all one thinks and says will be pure on one's fast-day.

The Bible here refers to the idea of the fast and not to starving the body, because the reference is not to fasts commanded in the Torah but to the individual fast about which it says 'Thou shalt not hide thyself from thine own flesh'. It is criticizing those who fix special fasts and frequently starve themselves, but are not concerned with afflicting their souls—and they are the ones who say 'Wherefore have we fasted and Thou seest not?' These men take no pride in observing the Biblical fasts, just as they take no pride in eating unleavened bread on the Passover or hearing the ram's horn on the New Year, but they take pride in afflicting themselves with a stringency not commanded in the Bible; they are proud of themselves before God and say 'Wherefore have we afflicted our soul and Thou takest no knowledge?' God tells them, that had they been feeding the hungry, it would have been more acceptable to Him than their starving themselves unnecessarily. According to His attribute of mercy—by virtue of which He has mercy on the hungry and thirsty and orders them to be fed—He does not want you to starve yourselves and has no pity for unnecessary affliction of the flesh. He has mercy on you for afflicting your soul by withholding it from the pleasures of this world, and commands you to take care not to starve your body excessively, just as you take care that others should not starve.

Philosophers say that the souls of the wicked are prisoners of their evil inclination and so if the wicked man who wishes to repent starves himself, he has done a good thing for which he will be rewarded inasmuch as he has humbled his stubborn inclination and caused his stubborn heart to suffer. This is not the case with the righteous, whose spirit and rational soul prevail over their evil inclination and who control their carnal desires; and *a fortiori* they have no need to afflict their flesh unduly when their strength diminishes in their old age but should take care of their body over which they have control and not starve and weaken it, unless for the sake of a commandment or something similar. God does not want you to starve or weaken your body but to humble the stubborn soul—and that is why He has commanded its affliction. If the body prevails over the soul, you are obliged to rescue the soul from the control of the body and its desires, but if the soul prevails, you are not to worry about the body. This is the meaning of the rabbinical dictum (*Keritot* 6b): 'Every fast where the transgressors of Israel do not afflict themselves is not accounted a fast'. The Torah says of the Nazirite (Numbers vi. 11): 'Make an atonement for him in that he sinned against his soul' to teach you that God is not worshipped through the body but through man's spirit and rational soul concentrating and meditating on the might and fear of God and grasping wisdom—viz., studying the Torah.

74

Because most men sin in their souls and do not realize their evil and fail to understand the proper way, the Rabbis have seen fit to encourage public fasts in times of drought and trouble in order to humble the stubborn hearts. The humble of spirit and crushed of heart will help them by his fasting and prayers which will lead to their prayers being heard along with his.

Scripture next expounds the reward accorded to each of the two above-mentioned categories for obeying the Divine commandments. It says (Isaiah lviii. 8): 'Then shall thy light break forth as the morning and thine health shall spring forth speedily and thy righteousness shall go before thee, the glory of God shall be thy rearward'. The first part of this verse refers to the man who is ruled by his evil inclination. It says to him; if you loose the bands of wickedness and undo the bands of the yoke (cf. verse 6), then 'thy light shall break forth as the morning', i.e., your light—viz., the reward for your deeds—will shine as the morning star which is connected with the advent of light in the world. 'And thine health shall spring forth speedily'; the remedy for the sickness of your evil inclination will spring forth speedily and you will find forgiveness and atonement. The latter part of the verse refers to the man who afflicts himself with bowing of head and spreading of ashes (cf. verse 5). It says to him: If you deal your bread to the hungry and bring the poor that are cast out to your house (cf. verse 7) then your righteousness will go before you in this world, and the glory of the Lord shall be your rearward in the world to come. By this action the iniquities of these men are forgiven and they are rewarded in the world to come; hitherto they had not been worthy to supplicate for Divine grace, but He is showing them the way by which their prayer can be heard.

It says to them (Isaiah lviii. 9): 'Then shalt thou call and the Lord shall answer; thou shalt cry and He shall say: Here I am. If thou take away from the midst of thee the yoke, the putting forth of the finger and speaking wickedness'. This verse is the wrong way round and has to be rearranged. If you take away from your midst the yoke, the putting forth of the finger and speaking wickedness, then you will call and the Lord will answer. This verse refers to the iniquities, transgressions and sins, teaching that man's prayer is not heard until he is purified of all three. 'If thou take away from the midst of thee the yoke', i.e., the iniquities in your heart, meaning that you must remove every impure thought and evil idea. 'The putting forth of the finger'—these are the sins, the action of the bodily members, meaning that no evil should be devised against your fellow-man either by you or by your agent. 'And speaking wickedness' refers to the transgressions of the mouth, meaning you shall not speak wickedness or lies against your people. The entire prohibition in this verse is clear and it praises him who heeds it as well as the previous verse; it shows that he who is guiltless before God is not complete until he is guiltless before His people, as it says (Numbers xxxii. 22): 'And be guiltless towards the Lord and towards Israel'. Then if he is guiltless before God and His people, his voice will be answered and his cry heard, as it says: 'Then shalt thou call and the Lord shall answer; thou shalt cry and He shall say: Here I am'. The Rabbis have said (*Mishnah Berakhot* iii. 8): 'Not every one who desires to assume a name may assume it'.[1] You can therefore say from this that not everyone is worthy to offer a private supplication to God, because God does not hearken to prayers according to the will of the one who is praying but according to God's own will, as it says (Psalms lxix. 14): 'But as for me let my prayer be unto Thee, O Lord, in an acceptable time'—a time that will be acceptable to you. And who knows if his prayer does not serve to recall his iniquity, as it says (I Kings xvii. 18): 'Thou art come unto me to bring my sin to remembrance?'

One of the sages has said: 'Let not your heart pour out your supplication to God concerning your sufferings, but bear them— perhaps they are there to save you from greater troubles'. As it says (Proverbs iii. 11): 'My son, despise not the chastening of the Lord, neither be weary of His reproof'. He should be like the pious Rabbi Nahum Ish Gamzo who, whenever a mischance occurred to him, said 'This also is for the best', because of his confidence that all God's decrees are for the best, as it says (Psalms cxlv. 9) 'His tender mercies are over all His works'. If he utters a

[1] i.e. not everyone has the right to consider himself superior to the masses in his piety.

supplication to seek forgiveness for his transgressions after he is contrite and repents of them, then he may lengthen his prayer—this is not like the case of the person who prays for the fulfilment of his worldly desires.

The next verse explains the reward of the sage who helps others through his wisdom and says (Isaiah lviii. 10) 'And if thou draw out thy soul to the hungry and satisfy the poor soul; then shall thy light arise in darkness, and thy gloom be as the noonday'. After expounding in the previous verse the reward of him who takes away 'from the midst of thee the yoke', it now explains the reward of the wise man who brings his wisdom to others. It says 'And if thou draw out thy soul to the hungry'—the 'hungry' being those who desire to learn Torah, who elsewhere are called 'thirsty', as it says, 'Ha, everyone that thirsteth, come ye to the waters' (Isaiah lv. 1). The 'thirsty' are those who have to be led in the path of faith and to be taught Torah, whereas the 'hungry' are those who believe in the Torah and their entire desire is to study it. The Torah is called 'corn' in Proverbs xi. 26—'he that withholdeth corn, the people shall curse him'. If belief in the Torah is called 'water' why is it called 'corn'? It is like the case of living beings, some of whom feed on water alone and do not need corn, but all who feed on corn require water; similarly in the case of those who study Torah, if their faith is not firm, their Torah will not avail them because Torah was not given only to study and teach, but also to observe and to perform, to study and teach. The one who observes and performs but does not teach is superior to the one who teaches but does not observe.

This verse refers to teaching the Torah to the believer, which is greater than teaching it to the non-believer. 'If thou draw out thy soul to the hungry' means draw out thy wisdom, because man's wisdom is the soul which distinguishes him from other animals. The explanation of 'draw out' here is 'give', like in Proverbs viii. 35: 'And drew forth favour of the Lord' which means that he helps with favour or that favour is given him by God. So this verse commands you to give wisdom to all who seek it.

It says here 'And satisfy the poor soul' and previously (verse 7) it said 'Is it not to deal thy bread to the hungry?' referring to the charity of giving bread to the hungry. Concerning the teaching of Torah, it says 'And satisfy the poor soul', i.e., you shall satisfy the soul that is poor in wisdom. If you do this, then the light of your wisdom shall shine in the darkness as it says, 'Then shall thy light arise in the darkness'—it will lighten the heart of the one who has been in the darkness; for the ignorant fool dwells in darkness, and all his deeds are dark—as it says (Ecclesiastes ii. 14): 'The fool walketh in darkness' and if you teach him wisdom, you will lighten his darkness. It says 'And thy gloom shall be as the noonday' referring to the wisdom in the heart of the wise; if he keeps it to himself and does not impart it, this wisdom will be as though it remained in gloom; but when he teaches it, it is revealed to all who seek it, and then it will be clear as the noonday sun.

As it is discussing the reward of teaching the Torah, it continues (Isaiah lviii. 11–12) 'And the Lord shall guide thee continually and satisfy thy soul in dry places and make strong thy bones; and thou shalt be like a watered garden and like a spring of water whose waters fail not; and they that shall be of thee shall build the old waste places; thou shalt raise up the foundations of many generations; and thou shalt be called the repairer of the breach, the restorer of paths to dwell in'. These two verses list four rewards for him who disseminates Torah:

(1) The first reward is that 'the Lord shall guide thee continually'; you will guide others for a limited period when you teach them, but God will guide you for an unlimited period (this is the meaning of 'continually'). This shows that the reward for teaching is eternal and is never forfeited; even if a man teaches Torah and then desists, he will be credited with his teaching and this will never be lost.

Most commandments do not endure once they have been performed, e.g., the tabernacle or the 'lulav' on the Feast of Tabernacles or eating unleavened bread on the Feast of Passover, etc.— these are dependent on a specific time and the obligation passes once the time is over. Neglect of the performance is accounted an iniquity and the person forfeits the reward to which he would have been entitled. But he who teaches wisdom brings something

78

enduring into the world, giving life to the human soul which otherwise is like a beast; if subsequently he fails to teach Torah to another person, he commits a transgression, but does not lose thereby the reward for his former action, on account of which he is established in the world and rewarded in the world to come. Everyone of understanding accepts this proof. Concerning it, the Bible says, 'And the Lord shall guide thee continually and satisfy thy soul in dry places and make strong thy bones' in place of the previous statement, 'and satisfy the poor soul'. It promises to satisfy his soul with splendour in the next world in place of the dry places in this world; he will receive a clear reward in the next world and his body will be strengthened, so that no worm or maggot should have power over it. This, then is the first reward granted by God to him who teaches His Torah.

(2) The verse next postulates another reward acquired in this world, saying, 'thou shalt be like a watered garden and like a spring of water, whose waters fail not'. As a watered garden produces fruit and pleasant plants and its waters do not fail but also irrigate other fields and vineyards; so with the waters of the Torah he irrigates and plants the seeds of wisdom and performs kindness towards the thirsty and the hungry; and the waters of his Torah and his wisdom gush forth and multiply. These are the two rewards conveyed in the first verse.

(3) The second verse says: 'They that shall be of thee shall build the old waste places; thou shalt raise up the foundations of many generations'. This world really endures because of mercy and justice and these can only be known through the Torah which explains their nature; when there is Torah in the world truth and justice are patent, and if the world is conducted accordingly, all will endure properly. He who spreads Torah and brings it to the masses causes the building of waste places and the raising of all the inhabited places so that the foundations laid in one generation will endure for the next generation, as long as wisdom—which is the foundation of the building—continues to be firmly established. This is the third reward.

(4) It says: 'Thou shalt be called the repairer of the breach, the restorer of paths to dwell in.' If the building is founded on wisdom,

its praise is ascribed not only to wisdom, but also to you who have interpreted it correctly. So that he who communicates his wisdom to his contemporaries is deserving of the four rewards: merit in the world to come; praise in this world; the glory of his teaching being seen through his disciples; and the maturing of the fruits of his wisdom.

This verse concludes the exposition of the various types who occupy themselves with this world, the description of the path they should follow and their reward in the world to come. Scripture now turns its attention to the greatest man before God—the one designated as 'humble of spirit', viz., the one who removes himself entirely from this world and all its affairs and desires. Throughout his life he refrains from contemplating worldly ways and accustoms himself so as not to be occupied by them.

The next verse expounds his conduct, saying (Isaiah lviii. 13) 'If thou turn away thy usage[1] from the Sabbath, from pursuing thy business on My holy day; and call the Sabbath a delight, and the holy of the Lord honourable; and shalt honour it, not doing thy wonted ways, nor pursuing thy business, nor speaking thereof'. The first Sabbath mentioned in this verse refers to the actual Sabbath day and ceasing from work in general, viz., from all his work and business (the root of the word for 'Sabbath' having various applications in Hebrew, e.g., in Joshua v. 12: 'and the manna ceased (*va-yishbot*) on the morrow', i.e., it ceased descending, as had been customary; in Job xxxii. 1—'So these three men ceased (*va-yishbetu*) to answer Job', or in Genesis viii. 22—'Day and night shall not cease (*yishbotu*)'.

The explanation of 'thy usage' is from *ragil*, i.e., a person getting accustomed to something. Alternatively, it could come from *regalim*, meaning 'steps', and then the meaning would be: if you turn away your customary steps which you wish to take, so as not to perform these things on My holy day when you devote yourself to serving Me. As it says: 'From doing thy pleasures on My holy day'—i.e., either on the day set aside for My holiness or else the day you make yourselves holy to Me.

'And call the Sabbath a delight.' Call the resting from work a

[1] Generally taken from *regel* as 'thy foot'.

delight (Heb. *oneg*) and do not call it an affliction (Heb. *inui*), as though hinting at the Day of Atonement when Israel afflicts itself and which God also called a Sabbath and connected with them, as it says (Leviticus xxiii. 32): 'Ye shall cease work on your Sabbath', applying to you alone; this will be your affliction but it will bring joy to your hearts. It says 'The holy of the Lord, honourable', i.e., what is separated and hallowed to the Lord should be honoured and precious to you. 'And shalt honour it not doing thy wonted ways'—not doing everything which man generally does for the sake of his bodily pleasure in this world.

It divides the way of men into two: the demand of the longing (Heb. *hefetz*) to find Him and the contemplation and speaking of His existence (Heb. *metziuto*). Both are applied on this day to the believer, as it says 'Nor pursuing (*metzo*) thy business (*heftzekha*) nor speaking thereof'—not to speak or think of anything connected with worldly affairs, but to concentrate all your speech and thought on the world to come and the fear of God. It might appear that this verse refers only to the Sabbath day and the Day of Atonement, but careful consideration will show that it does not refer solely to these two days as it does not speak about receiving a reward for the performance of one or two commandments, but it refers generally to the man who all his days is devoted to the worship of God, observing His commandments, walking in the right path, and rejecting the lusts of this world. His entire way of life leads him out of the prison of this world, and the Sabbath day for him is not an occasion for good food and pleasant garments, but his pleasures are meditation on the Divine law and comprehending Divine manifestations. That man calls the affliction of this world richness, and resting from its preoccupations and desires a delight; as it says: 'And call the Sabbath (i.e., the resting) a delight'. All his life he rests from evil and, in addition, on the Sabbath he rests from work; all his life he afflicts himself and keeps far from this-worldly affairs, but in addition, on the Day of Atonement, he afflicts himself by abstaining from food, drink and carnal pleasures.

It is about this man that the next verse (Isaiah lviii. 14) speaks: 'Then shalt thou delight thyself in the Lord and I will cause thee to ride upon the high places of the earth. And I will feed thee with the heritage of Jacob, thy father. The mouth of the Lord has spoken'. Because this man was resting from the affairs of this world for the glory of God and was subduing his mouth, tongue, hand and heart from all evil pleasures and mundane occupations —and in addition abstained from food and drink on the Day of Atonement—God brings him close to His glory and grants him the reward of delighting in Him as a son in his father, as it says 'Then shall thou delight thyself in the Lord'. For controlling his inclination and humbling his soul, God rewards him and raises him to ride on the high places of the earth and to be elevated above his contemporaries—just as the hills and mountains are elevated above the earth—as it says 'And I will cause thee to ride upon the high places of the earth'. And for his abstention from worldly delights, God feeds him with the splendour of His glory, which He bestowed as a heritage upon Jacob, as it says: 'And feed thee with the heritage of Jacob thy father'. And it says (Deuteronomy xxxii. 9): 'For the Lord's portion is His people; Jacob is the lot of His inheritance'.

These two verses show that God has provided a goodly heritage for our father Jacob in the world to come, and this is inherited by those of his descendants who are God-fearing and devoted to serving the Lord; as it says 'The heritage of Jacob thy father which (Heb. *ki*) the mouth of the Lord hath spoken', i.e., the heritage, which the mouth of the Lord spoke through His Torah to give to Jacob as an inheritance. The word '*ki*' in this verse means 'which'[1] as in the verse (Numbers xiv. 13): 'The Egyptians, from among which ('*ki*') Thou broughtest up that people'. It says 'heritage of Jacob' and not 'of Israel' or of any of the other patriarchs to indicate the rich reward bequeathed by Jacob, which is stored for his God-fearing descendants in the world to come. This shows the glory of the man who separates himself from this world in that he inherits God's heritage in the world to come, which is known as 'the heritage of Jacob'. It is in the name of Jacob and not of the other patriarchs—who were equal to him in merit—because of the saying (Genesis xxv. 27): 'A plain man dwelling in tents' which

1 Generally translated as 'for'.

shows that Jacob did not occupy himself with acquiring the objects of this world and was not nearly as wealthy as Abraham and Isaac but supported himself by his toil and wages. God twice tested him with exile—in his middle age to Haran, in his old age to Egypt—and promised that in the end He would bring him back to his land and deliver him, as it says (Genesis xlvi. 4): 'And I will surely bring thee up again'. So God has tested his descendants twice with exile and has promised to redeem them eventually, when they acknowledge His glory and renounce the iniquity of this world. As it says (Deuteronomy xxx. 1): 'And it shall come to pass, when all these things are come upon thee'—culminating in the arduous exile in which we live today—'And thou shalt call them to mind among all the nations whither the Lord, thy God, has driven thee', i.e., what I have commanded you to know, viz., that the Lord is God in heavens above and in the earth beneath—there is no other. It continues: 'And thou shalt return unto the Lord thy God and shalt obey His voice' by distancing yourself from this world and its pleasures; 'That then the Lord thy God will turn thy captivity and have compassion upon thee'—and His redemption will follow repentance. We must therefore enquire, with God's help, into the nature of that repentance which brings man to redemption.

PART THREE

How the sinner can be rescued from his wicked ways through contrition and repentance

---

IT SAYS: (Hosea xiv. 2) 'Return (Heb. *shuvah*) O Israel unto the Lord thy God; for thou hast stumbled in thy iniquity' and another verse (Malachi iii. 7) says: 'Return (*shuvu*) unto Me and I will return to you'. 'Returning' here refers to the one who returns to the worship of God and seeks forgiveness for his iniquities and sins, whether committed intentionally or unintentionally; it is also used of God returning to those who seek His mercy. Other verses say: 'But if the wicked will turn (*yashuv*) from all his sins that he hath committed and keep all My statutes and do that which is lawful and right' (Ezekiel xviii. 21) and (ibid., xviii. 24) 'But when the righteous turneth away (*u-veshuv*) from his righteousness and committeth iniquity and doeth according to all the abominations which the wicked man doeth'. 'Turning' in these verses is applied to both the righteous and the wicked; a man can turn from an evil or from a good way—there is no difference in linguistic usage. So we see that the Hebrew root *shav* has many meanings into which we must enquire so as to determine the meaning of real repentance (*teshuvah*, from the same root), which is man's contribution for his evil deeds. We will then be able to distinguish the truly penitent.

The verb *shav* in Hebrew and its derivatives can be explained in seven ways. (1) 'Turning from one way to another' (or one's heart turns from one thing to another). This is a common meaning, cf. 'Thy children shall return (*yashuvu*) to their own border' (Jeremiah xxxi. 17); 'the Lord turned (*shav*) not from the fierceness of His great wrath' (II Kings xxiii. 26); 'I returned (*shavti*) and saw under the sun (Ecclesiastes ix. 11); 'And turn away (*ve-shav*) from His fierce anger' (Jonah iii. 9); 'Then shall the dust return' (*va-yashav*) to the earth' (Ecclesiastes xii. 7). This is not transitive in the *Kal* conjugation, but only in the *Hiphil* conjugation, cf. 'to the prophet that brought him back (*heshivo*)' (I Kings xiii. 20); 'He shall restore (*ve-heshiv*) that which he embezzled' (Leviticus v. 23); 'And thou shalt restore it (*ve-hashivoto*) to him again' (Deuteronomy xxii. 2).

(2) 'Return' or making something return; e.g., 'The Lord thy God will turn (*ve-heshiv*) thy captivity' (Deuteronomy xxx. 3) which is like saying 'will cause your captivity to turn'; similarly 'Turn us (*shuvenu*) O God of our salvation' (Psalms lxxxv. 4); 'Behold I will bring again (*shav*) the captivity of Jacob's tents' (Jeremiah xxx. 18); 'Turn again (*shuvah*) our captivity, O Lord' (Psalms cxxvi. 4).

(3) 'Giving' or 'paying a debt' or 'exchanging' etc., cf. 'Let the trespass be recompensed (*ha-mushav*) unto the Lord even to the priest' (Numbers v. 8); 'And rendered (*ve-heshiv*) unto the King of Israel a hundred thousand lambs' (II Kings iii. 4). The difference between 'He shall restore that which he has embezzled' and 'let the trespass be recompensed', is that one is returning the thing itself to its owners, the other is bringing a substitute. 'And rendered unto the king of Israel' is like saying 'and gave'. So the meaning here differs from the other meaning in the *Hiphil* conjugation that we gave previously.

(4) 'Dwell', 'stay'; cf. 'When the Lord stayed (*be-shuv*) the captivity of Zion' (Psalms cxxvi. 1);[1] meaning making them stay. This is on the paradigm of *shivah* like *kimah*, and *shivah* comes from *shav*, just as *kimah* comes from *kam*. Similarly 'And if you will still abide (*shov*) in this land' (Jeremiah xlii. 10) which means, if you

[1] The verse is also explained in No. 6 below.

will still dwell in this land. Similarly 'I will dwell (*ve-shavti*) in the House of the Lord for ever' (Psalms xxiii. 6).

(5) 'Cleaving', i.e., constant attachment to a thing. The paradigm is mostly the doubling of the third root letter (i.e., the *Polel*); cf. 'he went on cleaving (*shovav*) in the way of his heart' (Isaiah lvii. 17), *shovav* deriving from *shav* just as *komam* derives from *kam*. And just as *komam* means an intensification of the establishment, so *shovav* is an intensification of the cleaving, determinedly remaining on the way and never going aside from it. It comes from the *Kal* conjugation, like (Jeremiah xxxi. 19) 'Surely after I cleaved (*shuvi*) I repented'; not meaning after I turned from iniquity, but after I persevered in my wickedness, I repented. 'After that I was instructed and I smote upon my thigh', after I understood my stubbornness, I smote upon my thigh. From this meaning comes 'For the persistence (*meshuvat*) of the simple shall slay them' (Proverbs i. 32) in that they do not turn from their simplicity.

(6) 'Settle in ease', 'dwelling securely', e.g., 'Return (*shuvah*) O Lord unto the many thousands of Israel' (Numbers x. 36) meaning 'make them settle in safety'. Similarly 'when the Lord caused the captivity of Zion to settle' (Psalms cxxvi. 1) He caused them to settle; and also 'He settleth (*yeshovev*) my soul' (Psalms xxiii. 3), i.e., He will keep it securely, making it delight in good deeds and leading it to righteousness.

(7) 'Repents' or turns away from iniquity and sins. It is on account of this meaning that we are discussing this verb. The meaning is the same as in the first usage, i.e., turning from something, but this is different as the turning is to the world to come and the ways of God.

A consideration of the subject shows that there are two kinds of repentance—that of the righteous man, who has erred accidentally, and that of the wicked man who regrets the sins he has committed wittingly. Another distinction that can be made is between complete and incomplete repentance. The definition of repentance is the regret of a man for his evil deeds and sins, the implication being that after he has committed the transgression, he repents and firmly observes the commandment he has transgressed. This applies whether it is committed intentionally or unintentionally—but there is this difference that repentance for an intentional sin involves confession, and this is not so in the case of the accidental transgression, which a man does not realize he is committing and which requires merely repentance and a request for forgiveness. Both types of penitents must believe in the commandments, which they had transgressed at the time of transgression; these are the ones principally called repentant. As to the transgressor who does not believe in the commandment before or during the transgression but only subsequently—after it has been made known to him—and then he repents of it, the term 'repentant' does not strictly apply and is only used loosely. He can be called a convert or a seeker of the way to faith but not a penitent; cf. the verse (Ezekiel xxxiii. 19): 'When the wicked man turneth (Heb. *u-veshuv*) and doeth judgment'—possibly this wicked man did not originally believe, but yet his faith is called repentance. All who seek the right way which they had not sought previously, are called penitent. This can be explained in a different way.

It says 'Return from the transgression', meaning turn from it after it has been committed. It could have been committed accidentally or intentionally. The latter cannot apply to one who believes in the commandments, but the former is equally applicable to believers and non-believers. The punishment and reward of both categories are not identical. The punishment for an accidental sin is much more lenient than for an intentional transgression, while the reward for a person who repents of an intentional sin is generally believed to be greater than that for repentance over an accidental transgression. The categories have in common the repentance after the action has been committed. Those who repent before committing the action are of two types:

(1) He who repents after contemplating the action and intending to perform it; such a person will only repent if he believes in the punishment for the transgression—he is tempted by his evil inclination, but God removes the temptation from him.

(2) He who repents of a sin without even contemplating it, i.e., he believes in general, but does not know the specific punishment.

88

Since he knows in general that there is punishment, he refrains from committing the transgression; and this is reckoned to him, as if his repentance were *post factum*.

These are the two categories of those who repent before committing the action, and according to the sages, they merit greater Divine reward than those who repent after having transgressed, because the former deserve only reward and are not liable for punishment, while with the latter it is a case of averting punishment. If God rewards him, it is out of His charity and not because he deserves a reward, inasmuch as the forgiveness of his transgression should suffice in itself.

So we see that there are three general categories of penitents. They are included in the five categories already described of those who go on the right way and those who deviate from it. These five are:

(1–2) The completely righteous. The first is the 'humble of spirit', whose rational soul prevails over his evil inclination from the day of his birth to the day of his death; this man is too holy to be called penitent. The second is the 'crushed of heart' who inclines to this-worldly desires, but subdues this inclination from his youth until his death. Inasmuch as he subdues his inclination, he can be called repentant and he is the most praiseworthy type of penitent.

(3–5) Those not completely righteous or not righteous at all; repentance here is applicable in two instances. The first repents of his transgression after having committed it and never repeats it; the second either does not repent entirely or repents but subsequently commits the transgression again. The third type is the completely wicked man who maintains his evil ways and never repents as long as he lives. Just as the first type—the completely righteous—is too holy to be called repentant, so the term 'repentant' is too holy ever to be applied to this last category. The repentant, then, are of three types: the first is completely righteous, the second middling, the third, evil. In this order, they can be found in the Book of Jonah.

The Book begins (Jonah i. 1–2): 'Now the word of the Lord came unto Jonah, the son of Amittai, saying: "Arise, go to Nineveh, that great city and proclaim against it; for their wickedness is come up before me". And Jonah rose up to flee to Tarshish away from the presence of the Lord and went down to Joppa . . . and the ship was like to be broken . . .'

Our first question is: Why did Jonah not obey the Divine command and perform his mission? All God-fearing believers should say that his intention was for good and not for evil, and that it never occurred to him to transgress God's word, but that his action was motivated by humility and sincerity. The comparison has been drawn with Moses to whom God said (Exodus iii. 10): 'Come now and I will send thee unto Pharaoh that thou mayest bring forth my people, the children of Israel, from Egypt' and who replied 'Who am I that I should go unto Pharaoh and that I should bring forth the children of Israel out of Egypt?' So Jonah reasons *a fortiori*: 'If Moses, who was sent to bring out the righteous from the iron furnace delayed until he was helped by his brother Aaron, how much more should I—deputed messenger to warn the wicked—delay until I see what God has to say to me further'.

It says 'And went down to Joppa (Heb. *yafo*)', i.e., he under-stood[1] the beauty (Heb. *yofi*) of the reason for the command. And since he found a ship leaving for Tarshish his intention was con-firmed and he immediately paid the passage and boarded. He wanted to go to Tarshish in order to get out of the land where God revealed Himself to His prophets and reach another land where He would not reveal Himself. Hence it says: 'To Tarshish away from the presence of the Lord', in the hope that God would accomplish His mission through another prophet. Jonah himself did not wish to be a messenger to the wicked. Hence Jonah, in leaving Joppa, should be classed among the righteous and the prophets.

But if his intentions were good, why was he punished? He was not punished for his good intentions, but because God ordered His prophets to warn the wicked; as He said to Ezekiel (Ezekiel xxxiii. 8): 'I said unto the wicked: wicked man, thou shalt surely die; if thou doest not speak to warn the wicked from his way, that wicked man shall die in his iniquity—but the blood will I

[1] Heb., 'went down to the knowledge of'.

90

require at thine hand. Nevertheless, if thou warn the wicked of his way to turn from it and he turns not from his way; he shall die in his iniquity but thou hast delivered thy soul'. So Jonah by this action, even though his intentions may have been good, failed to warn the wicked as he was commanded and for this he was liable for punishment. You might say that the quotation from Ezekiel refers only to warning Israelites—as it says (Ezekiel xxxiii. 7): 'So thou, son of man, I have set thee a watchman unto the house of Israel; therefore, when thou shalt hear the word at My mouth, warn them from Me' and regarding other peoples, the custom is different. I reply that, as God expressly said to Jonah, 'Arise, go to Nineveh, that great city and proclaim against it', he was obliged to warn them, failing which God could hold Jonah guilty of their blood, not for their sakes, but for the sake of the Divine Command which he had failed to fulfil. This is not to be compared with the action of Moses who answered God (Exodus iv. 13): 'O Lord I pray Thee, send by the hand of him whom Thou wilt send', because Moses was not being sent to warn the wicked Pharaoh, but to bring out the children of Israel and God in His mercy would have brought them out, even if Moses had not come to them. Generally, as soon as God sees wickedness, he punishes the sinners; as it says of Sodom (Genesis xviii. 21) 'I will go down now and see whether they have done altogether according to the cry of it, which is come unto Me' and that very day 'The two angels came to Sodom at even' (Genesis xix. 1). So in the case of Jonah, He said, 'For their wickedness is come up before Me' and immediately Jonah was made a Divine messenger. But because he delayed, he was punished, as it says (Jonah i. 4): 'The Lord hurled a great wind into the sea and there was a mighty tempest in the sea so that the ship was like to be broken'. When God is angry with His prophets and those who fear Him, He punishes them in the natural way of this world but when He delivers them, He employs miracles and supernatural means. This was the case with Jonah, where His anger was expressed by hurling a great wind and a mighty tempest into the sea, which is a natural phenomenon; but when it came to deliverance, it was by means of a great miracle.

91

When the sailors saw this tempest, they acted according to their customs, as it says (Jonah i. 5): 'And the mariners were afraid and cried, every man unto his God; and they cast forth the wares that were in the ship into the sea to lighten it unto them' as is customary, when the sea becomes stormy. However, these sailors did not have much faith in their gods because immediately after calling on them, they took the precaution of casting their wares into the sea, and did not continue to call on them. Jonah did not act thus, but accepted the Divine judgment and was confident of God's mercy, as it says 'But Jonah was gone down into the innermost parts of the ship; and he lay and was fast asleep'. When he saw the storm, it never occurred to him that he was its cause, for his intentions in fleeing to Tarshish were God-fearing and he was certain that God would deliver him, as He delivers all the righteous, as it says (Psalms xxxiv. 20): 'Many are the afflictions of the righteous, but the Lord delivereth him out of all'. So he slept securely and without fear, as it says 'and was fast asleep'.

It continues (Jonah i. 6): 'So the shipmaster came to him and said "What meanest thou, that thou sleepest? Arise, call upon thy God, if so be it that God will think upon us, that we perish not"'. This shipmaster was a wise person and said to Jonah: 'What do you mean by sleeping fearlessly? If you are sure of your righteousness and confident that God will have mercy on you, you must request His mercy to hasten His salvation. So arise and call upon your God; perhaps He will think upon us so that we will not perish', and he properly said to him, that all who are in trouble in this world can be delivered by prayer, as it says (Psalms xxxiv. 18): 'They cry and the Lord heareth them and delivereth them of all their troubles'. God hears the cry of all who are oppressed, as it says (Exodus xxii. 26): 'It shall come to pass when he crieth unto Me that I will hear; for I am gracious'. God in His graciousness and mercy hears all who cry to Him in trouble. So if a man has been robbed and patiently remains quiet, he receives the reward of his patience in the world to come and the robber is punished; but if he cries out to God, the robber is punished—unless he has made his peace with the robbed—but the robbed is not rewarded in the world to come because he has been appeased in this world. So we say that the shipmaster spoke wisely, and Jonah was silent and patient to increase his reward in the world to come.

Next we have to ask, whether Jonah called or not, when the shipmaster said 'Arise and call upon thy God'. If we examine the matter, we see that Jonah did not pray at that time, because he realized that he had been mistaken and it was proper for him not to pray but to remain silent, as it says (Lamentations iii. 28): 'He sitteth alone and keepeth silence because he has borne it upon him'. When God punishes those who fear him, they remain silent and acknowledge the justice of the judgment and the punishment of God is dear to them. So it says 'He lay and was fast asleep'—he went down inside the ship and was silent. Then the sailors, each of whom was calling to his god as the storm increased, went to look for the rest of the passengers to urge them to pray, as it says 'They said, everyone to his fellow: "Come, let us cast lots that we may know for whose cause this evil is upon us"', i.e., who is not praying to his god—perhaps he is the cause of this evil. 'So they cast lots and the lot fell upon Jonah'; they cast lots on everyone, whether he was praying or not, and the lot showed that each of them had been praying to his god and was afraid of the storm, except Jonah, as it says 'And the lot fell upon Jonah'. Then they said 'Tell us, we pray thee, for whose cause this evil is upon us', i.e., who is causing us this evil? They were trying to find out who was responsible. When they discovered that it was Jonah, they wanted to ascertain the cause of the misfortune, and asked 'What is thine occupation? And whence comest thou? What is thy country? And of what people art thou?' They asked him about four things—his work, his journey, his land and his people—in order to find out the cause of the evil that had befallen them. They first asked about his work, saying 'What is thine occupation?'—perhaps he was a magician or sorcerer and had caused this storm by sorcery. Then they enquired as to his route, saying 'Whence comest thou?'—perhaps he was a messenger for such evil men. Next they said 'What is thy country?'—perhaps he came from a bad country or from an area that they hated. Finally they enquired as to his people, saying 'Of what people art thou?—perhaps he came from an evildoing people?

He did not reply in the order of their questions, but answered their last query first, as it says 'He said unto them "I am a Hebrew" ', i.e., you need not be afraid of me, as I come from the people to whom any deed that can harm man is forbidden. 'I am a Hebrew' and nothing more, except that I am God-fearing, and God-fearing men do not usually meddle with evil, as it says 'I fear God, the Lord of Heaven, who has made the sea and the dry land'. Since it was clear to the sailors that Jonah could not be suspected of having done any evil they were afraid that the storm would increase in intensity and they would perish; as it says 'Then were the men exceedingly afraid', for they saw that the storm was on them alone. 'They said unto him: "Why have you done this?" ' The men knew that he had fled from the Lord, because he had told them; i.e., from what he had told them, they had realized that he was fleeing—not that he told them explicitly, but they deduced it from his words. He said to them 'For (*ki*) I fear God' and from this they understood, that he was fleeing. *Ki* in this verse is as in the verse (Proverbs xvi. 26): 'The soul of him that laboureth laboureth for himself, for (*ki*) his mouth brought iniquity (*akhaph*) upon him', i.e., his mouth is an iniquity to him. The word *akhaph* is from the same root as 'Neither shall my sin (*akhpi*) be heavy upon thee' (Job xxxiii. 7), meaning 'my iniquity' or 'my transgression'. The meaning of the verse in Proverbs is that the iniquity of the mouth of him that laboureth has caused labour to his soul, i.e., the iniquity of his mouth has caused it the labour. Similarly (II Chronicles xxii. 6) 'And he returned to be healed in Jezreel because of (*ki*) the wounds that were given him.' So you can see here that from what he told them, they knew that he was fleeing.

The sailors were therefore afraid that God had sent the storm on account of their sin in bringing him on board and accepting his passage money. 'They said unto him: What shall we do unto thee, that the sea may be calm unto us? The sea is getting stormier because we have brought you with us.' He answered that this storm was not on their account, but on his, saying unto them 'Take me up and cast me forth unto the sea; so shall the sea be calm unto you; for I know it is for my sake that this tempest is upon you'. When they heard him giving himself up to death, they were sorry for him and they said 'If we take him back where we came from, God could do what He wished and we would be innocent.' So it says 'Nevertheless the men rowed hard to bring it to land, but they could not; for the sea wrought and was tempestuous against them and they were unable to reach land'.

When they realized that they were unable to land, they sought God's mercy in two respects—to rescue them from the storm and to deliver them from iniquity, as it says 'They cried unto the Lord and said "We beseech Thee, O Lord, we beseech Thee, let us not perish for this man's life" '—if we retain him amongst us. 'And lay not upon us innocent. blood'—do not make us guilty of the murder of an innocent person if we cast him into the sea, inasmuch as he has delivered himself into Your hands; 'For Thou, O Lord, hast done as it pleased Thee'.

After they had stated their request and reasoning to God, they threw Jonah out of the ship, as it says, 'So they took up Jonah and cast him forth into the sea; and the sea ceased from His raging (mi-zaapo)', the sea ceased the raging caused by God, for the suffix of mi-zaapo refers to God, not to the sea. When there is a tempest, the Hebrew word is saar (storm), but here the word is zaaph (raging) which is used only of God, cf. Micah vii. 9: 'I will bear the raging of the Lord, because I have sinned against Him'. The sea was tempestuous because of the raging of God; when His rage stopped, the sea ceased to be tempestuous.

'And the men feared the Lord exceedingly and offered a sacrifice unto the Lord and made vows'. There is a big difference between the 'fear' in this context and that mentioned previously, when it said: 'Then were the men exceedingly afraid and said to him "Why has thou done this?" ' The first fear was of events in this world, and the latter was fear of heaven and of the punishments of the world to come and implied repentance to the proper path. As it says 'And offered a sacrifice unto the Lord', i.e., they believed in His Torah at that time and they humbled their hearts and their inclinations, and this was reckoned as though they had made a sacrifice, as it says (Psalms li. 19): 'The sacrifices of God are a broken spirit, a broken and contrite heart'. It is not correct to say

95

that they offered actual sacrifices in mid-sea; moreover, they were not familiar with the sacrificial laws. It says 'And made vows' in that they agreed always to maintain their God-fearing ways when they returned to their lands.

So we have two types of penitence, as mentioned at the outset of our explanation. The first is the repentance of the perfectly righteous man, viz., Jonah; the second is the repentance of the wicked men, viz., the sailors, who were saved from punishment by their prayers and repentance. It is obvious that had Jonah prayed and sought mercy, his prayer would have been heard; but he did not wish to pray until he had received God's punishment for the sin he had committed unwittingly. He knew that God would not punish him with death, but would chastise him with severe trials, as it says: 'Now the Lord had prepared a great fish to swallow up Jonah. And Jonah was in the belly of the fish for three days and three nights'. The great fish was not great corporeally, for there were many bigger fish in the sea and its superiority was not in this respect. It was great in age and in merit; in age, because it had been designated for this action since the six days of creation, and in merit, because it was to save the soul of a righteous man. It says 'to swallow up (Heb. *li-veloa*) Jonah', i.e., to hide or cover up Jonah, cf. Numbers iv. 20 'To see a sanctuary lest they be swallowed (*kevalla*)' meaning 'covering' or 'hiding'. The word *li-veloa* is written defectively (without a *vav*) to indicate that he had already been swallowed.

It says 'to swallow up Jonah' where it could have said 'And it swallowed up Jonah', as later in the Book (iv. 6) it says 'The Lord God prepared a gourd and made it to come up over Jonah, that it might be a shadow over his head to deliver him from his evil', i.e., as soon as it was designated for this purpose, it came up. But here it does not say 'The Lord had prepared a big fish to swallow and it swallowed up', so that none should think that God designated the fish on the spot to swallow him up; it says 'to swallow up' to show that it had been long since prepared for this deed. It can also be said that it is written 'To swallow up' because God gave the fish no power to harm Jonah or prevail over him; no animal can have dominion over man, so how can a fish prevail over a righteous man? This shows that God caused him to be swallowed up by the fish and hid him there.

'And Jonah was in the belly of the fish for three days and three nights.' For three whole days Jonah was being reprimanded by the Lord and was not able to pray because of his great shame. These three days correspond to the three days of darkness in Egypt, and just as God brought the children of Israel out of Egypt after three days of darkness, so He brought Jonah out of the belly of the fish after three days of darkness. It says 'three days and three nights' with days preceding nights, although in the order of creation night came first; this is for the sake of the comparison with the three days in Egypt.

Just as the Israelites lived in light all three days—day and night—while knowing which were the night periods, as it says (Exodus x. 23): 'But all the children of Israel had light in their dwellings', i.e., they even had light in the hours of darkness—so Jonah lived all three days and nights in light in the belly of the fish, although he knew which were the night periods. This is why it puts 'days' before 'nights'. Once Jonah knew that three full days had passed corresponding to the number of the days of darkness in Egypt he felt confident that God would save him and thereupon he began to pray, as it says in the next verse: 'Then Jonah prayed unto the Lord his God out of the belly of the fish (Heb. *dagah*)'. In the previous verse, it said 'In the belly of the fish (*dag*)'. The difference in the terms shows that when Jonah entered the fish, it was alive, but when he reached its belly, it was dead, because it had been designated since the days of creation solely for the purpose of swallowing Jonah. Once this was done, its purpose was fulfilled and it died and was called *dagah* cf. Exodus vii. 21: 'And the fish (*dagah*) that was in the river, died'—in both contexts *dagah* refers to dead fish.

In this connection, Jonah says in his prayer 'I cried by reason of my affliction unto the Lord and He heard me; out of the belly of Sheol cried I and Thou heardest my voice', i.e., from the belly of the dead fish, which was in Sheol, I cried; for living in the body of a dead object is like living in the belly of Sheol. This in itself was a miracle, because naturally a dead fish would come to the surface and float, but the fish in which Jonah was, remained submerged in the depths, as it says 'For Thou hast cast me into the deep in the midst of the seas', because he had reached the bottom of the depths.

It says 'The river encompassed me about' because the streams enter the sea, but do not reach its depths. Since Jonah was in the depths, the streams were around him outside on every side and the waves were passing him by in every direction as it says 'All Thy billows and Thy waves passed over me; then I said I am cast out of Thy sight; yet will I look again towards Thy holy Temple; the waters compassed me about even to the soul; the depths closed me roundabout, the reeds were wrapped about my head'. It can be asked why the Red Sea[1] should be connected with the depths rather than any other sea. If the order of these two verses is rearranged, they become comprehensible. 'Then I said I am cast out of Thy sight, when the waters encompassed me about even to the soul', i.e., when the waters of the deep were surrounding me on every side, I said that I am cast out of Thy sight. But when I saw 'the reeds were wrapped around my head', i.e., were like a bandage at the back of my head, then I said 'I will look again towards Thy holy Temple'. The Red Sea is west of the Land of Israel and its waters were wrapping around his head from the back and he was facing the Land of Israel, and so was confident, that God would grant him the privilege of seeing His Temple.

It can also be said that when he saw the waters of the Red Sea above his head, he recalled the great miracle wrought by God for his ancestors in dividing the Red Sea and he felt sure that God would bring him out of the sea and let him see the Temple. It says 'I went down to the bottom of the mountains; the earth with her bars closed upon me for ever'. The word 'bottom' is a measure; i.e., as the mountains are high upon the earth, so was the extent of the depths below the sea. It says 'the bars (berihei) of the earth were about me for ever'. The bars of the earth are like lines passing through the middle of the earth to the point which in Arabic is called 'markazun' (the centre). The line which passes through this point comes out to the surface of the earth on both sides and it is

[1] Literally 'The Sea of Reeds'.

98

driven out (*mavriah*) from one extremity to the other. This is the line that is called the bar; it is longer than a straight line that is passing through the earth and divides it. The point which is called the centre is below all other points on the earth, and all lines called 'bar' pass through it. Jonah shows by these words that he had reached the extremities of the depths and the bottom of the earth. He says 'The earth with its bars was around me', i.e., he was in the middle of the earth, through which all the bars pass. He said 'About me for ever' meaning a bar from every possible side of the world was passing through, as happens whenever one is at the centre of a circle or a sphere. It continues 'Yet has Thou brought up my life from corruption O Lord, my God'—You bring me up out of this great tribulation. 'When my soul fainted within me, I remembered the Lord', i.e., when my soul faints and weeps because of my many troubles and remembers God, at that time Thou in Thy mercy raisest me for the merit of my prayer, as it says 'My prayer came in unto Thee into Thy holy Temple'. From this it can be learned that God is merciful and gracious to whomsoever is troubled and remembers God, seeking His mercy with all his soul, with complete devotion and repentance; as it says (Deuteronomy iv. 29): 'But from thence thou wilt seek the Lord thy God; and thou shalt find Him, if thou search after Him with all thy heart and with all thy soul', i.e., when you seek God from thence, viz., from the places of your exile, you will find His mercy when you seek Him with all your heart and soul.

It says (Psalms xxxii. 5) 'I made known my sin unto Thee and mine iniquity have I not hid. I said I will confess my transgressions unto the Lord; and Thou forgavest the iniquity of my sin. Selah.' This shows, that confessions of sins should be made at the time of repentance, and God forgives them. It also indicates how confession should be made. First, a man makes known his sins, i.e., wrong deeds, as it says 'I made known my sin unto Thee'; it says 'made known', as deeds are obvious. Next it says 'and my iniquities have I not hid'—these are evil thoughts which remain hidden if they are not revealed. And next 'I will confess my transgressions', i.e., evil words, and he uses the verb for oral confession to show that the reference is to evil speech. It puts sins before

99

transgressions as it goes from the lighter to the more serious. A bad action unaccompanied by thought or speech is the least serious—because it can under no circumstance be looked upon as wilful—it is accidental. Evil thought alone—not translated into action or speech—is more serious than merely wrong deeds, as it can be of idol-worship, which would not be possible in the case of a deed without corresponding thought. Evil speech is more serious than either of these two, even if unaccompanied by action or thought, because it involves profanity of the Divine Name and the mention of false gods. It is also more serious than evil thought alone, although in the case of evil thought we are afraid of idol worship, because speech is actualized and is heard, whereas thought can be neither seen nor heard. The verse then starts with the less serious and proceeds to the more serious, as the rabbis have pointed out. It shows the order of confession—that God accepts such repentance and confession, from the lesser to the greater, as it says: 'And Thou forgavest the iniquity of my sin. Selah.'

We now must explain why it only refers to iniquities and sins, as it says 'the iniquity of my sin' and does not mention transgressions. Two answers have been propounded, one taking the omission to indicate leniency, and the other stringency.

(1) The former answer points out that the verse says 'Thou forgavest the iniquity of my sin', linking iniquity with sin. Had it said 'My iniquity and my sin', it would have mentioned each one separately, but it does not do so, because a man is not punished or required to make a confession for an evil thought which is not actualized or for a bad deed which is not premeditated and intentional. In these instances, regret for the deed or the thought is sufficient. Similarly, man is not punished for wrong speech that is not deliberate. The verse says 'the iniquity of my sin', to connect the two, i.e., wrong action after an evil thought, or evil thought dependent on a wrong action, which require atonement and forgiveness. But it does not say 'iniquity of transgression' or 'transgression of iniquity', because what is spoken comes from the mouth, just as other deeds are the actions of other limbs. And as it has mentioned 'the iniquity of sin', which is evil thought—and includes the bad deed in that expression which means the evil

action of the mouth—the Bible does not need to go further into the subject. This is the lenient view.

(2) The stringent answer is that all impure thoughts and unworthy actions, whether important or not, are atoned for by repentance, regret and confession to God. But this is not the case with the transgression of the mouth. For from the lightest such offence such as mentioning the Divine Name in an unworthy place, to the most serious such as taking a false oath—repentance and confession do not atone, until punishment has been exacted in the world to come, as it says (Exodus xx. 7): 'For the Lord will not hold him guiltless who takes His name in vain.' Hence all the righteous and pious take care not to mention a Divine Name or attribute by way of an oath, etc., fearing that they might thereby commit an iniquity, which cannot be atoned for by repentance.

The Bible continues (Psalms xxxii. 6): 'For this shall everyone who is godly pray unto Thee, in a time when Thou mayest be found; surely, when the great waters overflow, they will not reach unto him', i.e., this is the way all the godly pray to You, when finding mercy with You. It says 'everyone who is godly, prays' and not 'all who pray', because not all who confess their sins are worthy of this, but only the godly, namely—according to this verse—those who are careful not to transgress with their mouth. The first verse shows that the repentance of the one who has been careless about uttering the Divine Name or attributes in an oath is incomplete. Since the second verse mentions the godly, it follows that he who is not careful about mentioning the Divine Name is not godly. These two verses teach us also the way of fear and repentance, and the correct prayer of the godly. This is that the godly, who knows that he has never been lax in mentioning the Divine Name, confesses his sins, transgressions and iniquities, and can pray in the confidence that his prayer will be favourably received and that he will be spared all sorrow—and should the waters of the sea overflow, they would not reach him, as it says 'When the great waters overflow, they will not reach unto him'. As Jonah said: 'When my soul fainted within me, I remembered the Lord and my prayer came in unto Thee into Thine Holy Temple', i.e., when my soul was faint and supplicating, I remembered my God with upright heart and complete devotion and at once I knew that my prayer had been heard, as it says, 'My prayer came in unto Thee into Thine holy Temple'.

After that, he says 'They that observe lying vanities forsake their own mercy' and it says 'But I will sacrifice unto Thee with the voice of thanksgiving; I will pay that which I have vowed; salvation is of the Lord'. He said to God: 'If You had mercy on the sailors, who were idol worshippers, because they renounced their disgraceful actions and accounted this to them as if they had offered sacrifices and pronounced vows'—as it says 'And offered a sacrifice to the Lord and made vows'—and they did not believe they would fulfil their vows—then how much more I, who acknowledge Your Torah and set my prayer as a sacrifice before You, as it says, 'I will sacrifice unto Thee with the voice of thanksgiving; I will pay that which I have vowed'—that I will be worthy to find Your great salvation, as it says: 'Salvation is of the Lord'. God in His many mercies rewarded his intent and accepted his prayer, answering him immediately, as it says: 'The Lord spake unto the fish (la-dag) and it vomited out Jonah upon the dry land'. You see from here that the fish which had swallowed Jonah into its belly was dead, and God revived it for Jonah's sake or life entered it with the light of salvation that came to Jonah, and hence it was again called dag as originally. It says 'And vomited out Jonah', i.e., it vomited him out immediately. It does not say 'to vomit out Jonah'—as it said 'to swallow Jonah' in the first verse—because all living things are destined to serve and benefit the righteous and are not permitted to harm them. The fish by its former action—had it been completed—would have harmed Jonah but by its latter act it benefited him and was useful in serving him.

When Jonah came out on to dry land, he immediately prophesied, as it says the second time: 'The word of the Lord came unto Jonah, saying "Arise, go unto Nineveh, that great city and preach unto it the preaching that I bid thee"'. It says 'a second time', meaning second to the former prophecy—i.e., another time. Or you can say it means another subject, because this prophecy is not like the preceding one, for the first did not allow for the repentance of the men of Nineveh but provided for their immediate punishment; it was only with the second prophecy that the possibility of repentance was opened before them and the execution of the Divine Judgment delayed. The evidence for this is in the first prophecy which says 'And cry against it for their wickedness is come up before me'; i.e., he should decree the fate of those whose wickedness had come up before God and that is their destruction from the world; as it is said of Sodom (Genesis xix. 13): 'Behold, the cry of them is waxen great before the face of the Lord; and the Lord hath sent us to destroy it'. Hence the men of Nineveh would have been destroyed had that prophecy been fulfilled. But in the second prophecy it says 'Preach unto it the preaching that I bid thee'—that I am going to bid you—and the gates of repentance will be opened before them during this respite. In the first prophecy it says 'Cry against it' (*aleha* from *al*) and in the second it says 'Cry to it' (*eleha* from *el*). Crying sometimes has bad implications as it says 'He hath called an assembly against me' (*alay*) (Lamentations i. 15), and sometimes good, as (Ezekiel xxxvi. 29) 'And I will call for (*el*) the corn and increase it.' You will find throughout that the second prophecy is more lenient than the first; and the meaning of a 'second time' at the beginning of the second prophecy means 'other'. It says 'So Jonah arose and went to Nineveh according to the word of the Lord'. He went to fulfil the word of the Lord in the latter mission, of which it says 'That I bid thee'. And it says 'Now Nineveh was an exceeding great city to God, a three days' journey', i.e., its size could not be measured by human, but only by Divine standards. This Nineveh had three sister towns in the world—Rehoboth next, then Resen, and Calah the smallest, as it says (Genesis x. 10–11) 'And builded Nineveh and Calah, the same is a great city', i.e., between Nineveh the great city and Calah the small one.

It says 'Jonah began (*vayahel*) to enter into the city a day's journey'; as he journeyed all that day he was waiting for (*meyahel*) the word of the Lord which had been promised to him—'Preach unto it the preaching that I bid Thee'. He did not know what it was until the beginning of the second day, when it became clear to him, as it says 'He cried and said: Yet forty days and Nineveh will be overthrown'. But the preaching was delayed for a day, so that he could reach the centre of the city in order that the trustworthiness of his message should be clear to the men of Nineveh as he came amongst them. We can also say that the preaching was after one day's journey, so that those who passed back to the entrance of the city as well as those who ran ahead to the other extremity would be able to report the message of the preaching. So that only on the third day was the preaching heard through the length of the three days' journey and people ran ahead of him in terror to relate his message.

His preaching lasted for forty days, corresponding to the forty days that it rained upon the earth during the Flood period. This shows that the wickedness of the men of Nineveh is comparable with that of the Flood generation. And just as it was said of the Flood generation (Genesis vi. 5) 'The wickedness of man was great in the earth' so it was said of the men of Nineveh 'For their wickedness is come up before Me'. You can say that their wickedness was as great as that of the Flood generation, because the latter was over the entire earth, as it says: 'The wickedness of man was great in the earth' and the wickedness of the men of Nineveh reached on high, as it says (Jonah i. 2) 'For their wickedness is come up before Me'. God granted a stay to Nineveh—but He did not give the Flood generation the opportunity of delay because every living thing in all the earth in that generation lived a corrupt life, whereas with the men of Nineveh, they alone were doing evil. When they heard the preaching, they believed it, as it says 'So the people of Nineveh believed in God', and even though their faith was not perfect, they believed that He could fulfil what was preached. All nations who do not fear God call on His name as was the case with the sailors—even before they comprehended the fear of God, it says 'Then the men feared God exceedingly'. So we say that the faith of the men of Nineveh was not perfect and in three respects the fear of the sailors was superior:

(1) Fear is greater than faith according to its prime meaning because faith implies seeing that a thing is true and correct. But if the thing is valueless, it is as it says (Proverbs xiv. 15): 'The simple believeth everything', i.e., whether it be true or false, and it is

known that not everything is true, and most things contain lies and falsehoods, but the simple cannot distinguish between them—he believes all, while the wise man can discern in what he ought to believe. So the simple and the wise are both called believers although there is a great difference between them. This shows that fear came to the world after faith, because fear without faith is incomplete; but this is a conditional fear and is called 'dread' or 'fright' etc., and is not fit to be called actual 'fear' as fear proper depends on a preceding faith. Since it says about the sailors 'The men feared the Lord' we call them fearing and believers, because fearing only follows faith. But we do not call the men of Nineveh 'fearing'—even though they had faith—, because they believed without being God-fearing. This then is the first superiority of the sailors over the men of Nineveh.

(2) The second is that it says of the sailors 'Then the men feared the Lord exceedingly' and of the men in Nineveh 'They believed in God'. The Bible shows that the fear of the sailors was great but it has nothing to say of the faith of the men of Nineveh.

(3) Of the sailors, it says, 'They feared the Lord' linking their great fear and repentance to the Divine Name 'the Lord' which is used when He sits on the throne of kindness, mercy, righteousness, glory and kingship, and this Name is uniquely His, not shared with any worldly creation. But of the men of Nineveh it says 'They believed in God', connecting their faith with the name *Elohim* used of God when He sits on the throne of judgment, and used equally of God and human judges.

The men of Nineveh believed that God would punish them and exact retribution from them—just as every king and potentate can punish his subjects—and because of their terror rather than their upright faith 'they proclaimed a fast and put on sackcloth from the greatest of them even to the least of them', i.e., to weep and mourn for themselves because of the terror of the punishment about to befall them in this world, and not out of fear or perfect faith. The faith of the men of Nineveh commenced on the day Jonah began preaching, as it is mentioned immediately after the preaching 'He cried and said: "Yet forty days and Nineveh shall be overthrown"'... And the people of Nineveh believed God and they proclaimed a fast and put on sackcloth, from the greatest of them even to the least of them'.

On that day the tidings did not reach the king of Nineveh—perhaps the royal palace was at one extremity of the city and Jonah came in at the other side, and began to preach on the second day; but word did not reach the king until the third day. As it says 'And the tidings reached the king of Nineveh as he arose from his throne; and he laid his robe from him, covered him with sackcloth, and sat in ashes'. The tidings that reached him were that the men of Nineveh had called a fast and donned sackcloth and he did likewise. So the king followed the advice of the people of the city, as it says 'He caused it to be proclaimed and published through Nineveh by the wisdom of the king and the nobles', on the advice of the king and the advice of the nobles of the city and not out of fear of God.

It says (Jonah iii. 7) 'Persons nor beasts, herds nor flocks; let them not feed nor drink water.' 'Persons' here refers to the young, the sucklings and the babes who know nothing, as it says at the end of the prophecy (Jonah iv. 11): 'More than six score persons that cannot discern between their right hand and their left hand.' Just as these are the 'persons' later on, so in this verse the 'persons' are the young and the sucklings who cannot distinguish between good and evil. All those capable of understanding were already fasting and wearing sackcloth of their own free will, as it says 'And they put on sackcloth from the greatest of them even to the least of them'. There remained the sucklings and young children and the king on his initiative and that of his nobles proclaimed that they should not eat or drink, as it says 'Let them not taste anything'. This verb refers to both eating and drinking, i.e., they should taste neither food nor drink. Each is then enumerated individually. 'Let them not feed on anything', viz., food; 'nor drink water', viz., liquid. An alternative explanation is that 'Let them not taste' refers to man; 'let them not feed' to animals, 'let them not drink water' to both. According to this explanation 'let them not taste' refers to food alone, as it says (Job xii. 11): 'And will his palate taste his meat?', i.e., tasting is done only by the palate, and it is food that the palate and no other part of the body tastes.

106

It says 'Let man and beast be covered with sackcloth'—all living things should act identically as regards food, drink and clothing. It continues 'And cry mightily to God'; the children and animals, whom he has ordered to starve themselves and to don sackcloth, 'should cry mightily' to the Judge of the world—as a result of the king's advice and not out of faith because beasts and sucklings have not the intelligence to call on God out of fear or faith or knowledge, but they yell and howl, when they are in straits. You cannot deduce from this verse that it was the men of Nineveh who were calling on God or praying, but their entire plan was to afflict the children and the animals who know nothing and are innocent—so that God would have mercy on the city for their sakes. The men did not pray because it was their custom not to pray and they had no trust in their prayers on account of the greatness of their iniquities. Those who judge them favourably, say that they did not pray as they were ashamed to turn to heaven because of the multitude of their sins.

The conclusion of the proclamation ordered by the king in the city reads 'Let them be covered in sackcloth, both man and beast, and let them cry mightily unto God; yea, let them turn every person from his evil way and from the violence that is in their hands'. Since it says here 'every person from his evil way', it follows that 'man' mentioned at the beginning of the quotation ('man and beast') refers to children and sucklings and all who are not called 'person'. It says 'Every person from his evil way', i.e., from the life he was wont to lead. 'And from the violence that is in their hands' they should restore to their proper owners everything in their possession that had been stolen or obtained by violence.

Next it shows their motives, saying: 'Who can tell if God will turn and repent and turn away from His fierce anger that we perish not?' Their request was not to perish from this world, and God did not deem them worthy to seek forgiveness and atonement. Their request even began questioningly—'Who can tell if He will turn and repent?'—who knows whether or not He will turn and repent—because they had no confidence that the decree issued against them would be annulled as a result of their repentance. Nevertheless, the all-merciful God did not hide His face from them, as it says: 'God saw their works, that they turned from their evil way; and God repented from the evil He had said that He would do unto them; and He did it not'. God (*elohim*) sitting on His throne of judgment—cf. 'Unto the judges (*elohim*) shall come the cause of both of them' (Exodus xxii. 8)—saw their action in bringing every living thing worthy of mercy to cry out to Him, and that they had repented and turned from their violence. 'And God repented'—this repentance was in the nature of this-worldly justice and judgment, just as their repenting from their evil ways was for the sake of this world and not for the world to come. It does not say 'And the Lord repented' to show that there was no question of forgiveness for the world to come, which comes through the Divine attribute of mercy.[1]

There are two types of repentance by sinners (apart from the most exalted type of repentance—that of the righteous—which is a class by itself). One of these acquires life in this world, the other acquires both life in this world and forgiveness in the world to come. About this latter type, the Bible (Isaiah lv. 7) says: 'Let the wicked forsake his way and the unrighteous man his thoughts; and let him return unto the Lord and He will have mercy upon him, and to our God, for He pardons abundantly.' Repentance is mentioned here after his way and his thoughts. 'His way' refers to bad deeds and 'his thoughts' are evil meditations. Then it says: 'Let him return unto the Lord and He will have mercy upon him; and to our God, for He pardons abundantly'—that his repentance is for the sake of Divine mercy and He will have mercy upon him; 'and to our God' sitting on the throne of judgment that He who pardons abundantly, should pardon him.

There are three prerequisites for the acceptance of the repentance of the wicked: (1) ceasing wicked actions; (2) stopping impure meditation and speech in the heart and mouth; and (3) that both (1) and (2) should be for the sake of heaven. You find all this in the repentance of the crew of the ship. They acted for the sake of heaven, as it says: 'The men feared the Lord exceedingly'. The verse 'And offered a sacrifice to the Lord', shows that they

---

[1] Conveyed in the Divine Name 'the Lord'.

repented for their actions, as sacrifice implies action and 'sacrifice to the Lord' proves that it was for the sake of heaven. While the phrase 'and made vows' covers both the words of the mouth and the meditation of the heart. Hence they were worthy to be considered as the superior type of repentant wicked, worthy of forgiveness.

Concerning the incomplete repentance of the wicked, Scripture states (Ezekiel xviii. 23): 'Have I any pleasure at all that the wicked should die? saith the Lord God; and not that he should return from his ways and live?' If God decrees death for the wicked on account of his evil ways, the decree is conditional and is cancelled in the event of repentance as a result of which he lives out his full days as decreed at his birth; as it says 'He should return from his ways and live', viz., the lifespan originally destined for him.

Another verse (Ezekiel xxxiii. 11) says: 'As I live, saith the Lord God, I have no pleasure in the death of the wicked; but that the wicked turn from his way and live'. Up to this point, this verse is similar to the one quoted previously—both refer to the wicked among the nations of the world. But the conclusion of the second verse refers to the wicked in Israel, saying, 'Turn ye, turn ye from your evil ways; for why will you die, O House of Israel?' Repentance here is mentioned twice and in the first verse only once ('He should return from his ways and live') to show that the wicked in Israel are deserving of forgiveness in the world to come only when their repentance comprises two things—that they turn from their evil ways and that their repentance is for the sake of heaven; if both of these are fulfilled, they will be rewarded for their repentance in the world to come. When the wicked of the nations of the world repent of their ways, they acquire life in this world—which was the object of their repentance—but because they did not repent for the sake of heaven, they have no portion in the world to come. In this respect it says: 'Why will you die, O House of Israel?', i.e., why will you die a death for which you will be punished in the world to come? Concerning the repentance of the wicked, it says, 'That the wicked turn from his way and live', i.e., live in this world. It does not say he will repent and will not die, because with the wicked of the nations of the world—whether they repent or not—their death is one of perdition from this world and the world to come. But it does not say of Israel 'Turn from your ways and live' because their repentance is not for the sake of life in this world.

The life of the righteous in this world is not called a period of life, but of temporary sojourning and of terror. Proof of this is from the patriarch Jacob who, when asked by Pharaoh 'How many years is thy life?' (Genesis xlvii. 8), replied 'The days of the years of my sojourn . . . are few and evil', not answering 'the days of my life', as he was asked in Pharaoh's question. The verse concludes: 'And have not attained unto the days of the years of the life of my fathers in the days of their sojourning'. He calls the days of his life and that of his fathers 'days of sojourning', because the righteous live both in this world and the world to come, but their true life, which has permanence, is in the world to come, and their life in this world is to acquire sustenance, viz., merits for the world to come. They call this life 'days of sojourning' and they are terrified that the sustenance will be inadequately prepared.

You might think that the life of Israel in this world is called 'life' because of the verse (Ezekiel xviii. 32): 'For I have no pleasure in the death of him that dieth, saith the Lord God; wherefore turn yourselves, and live.' You could say that 'him that dieth' refers to the dead of the nations of the world and of Israel, and that since at the end it says, 'wherefore turn yourselves and live', you might deduce that the reference is to the life of this world for both Israel and the other nations, and that therefore the life of this world is called 'life' for Israel. But I say that 'him that dieth' refers solely to robbers and similar criminals—because robbery, etc., are the only crimes for which penitence alone does not suffice but has to be accompanied by restitution, to the owner, the next-of-kin, or to God—as is explained in the Torah. He is called 'him that dieth' because if he is from the nations of the world he is doomed to perdition, and if he is an Israelite, his death will not atone for the iniquity because of the stolen article, which remains in his possession, and for which he is punished after his death so that he dies in this world and is punished in the world to come. This is why it says '(Re-)turn yourselves and live'—he should return the stolen article and live. If the robber is an Israelite and he returns the stolen article, he completes the days of his sojourning in this world and acquires life in the world to come without punishment for his iniquity; while if he belongs to the nations of the world, he will live his life out in this world and not die prematurely like his fellows.

Concerning a stolen article it says elsewhere (Ezekiel xviii. 30): 'Return ye and turn yourselves from all your transgressions' to show that there are transgressions for which repentance alone atones, viz., all wrongs against God; and there are those which require repentance and restitution, e.g., robbery, theft and similar transgressions against a fellow-man. It says 'Turn from all your transgressions' 'transgressions' meaning wrongdoing by speech while robbery and theft are wrong actions. It could have said 'from all your sins', but it says 'from all your transgressions', so as to include such wrongs as robbery or shaming a fellow-man either in public or in private, which are not pardonable until the person wronged has been appeased. Hence the verse speaks generally, saying 'from all your transgressions' to include 'verbal robbery' with practical robbery. It calls them 'transgressions', because verbal robbery before God is more serious than robbery of money.

Now consider how great is the merit of restoring lost or stolen objects and of him, who seeks forgiveness for having stolen them—because for that alone God annulled the decree of destruction which Jonah had preached to the people of Nineveh. And Jonah was grieved at the non-fulfilment of his prophecy, as it says, 'It displeased Jonah exceedingly and made him very angry' (Jonah iv. 1) as he could not understand why his prophecy was not realized, 'And he prayed (va-yitpallel) unto the Lord'. This prayer was not a request for mercy, but comes from the root pelilah meaning that he asked a verdict from God. He said 'I pray Thee, O Lord, was not this my saying when I was yet in mine own country? When I was in mine own country, I knew that Thou wert a gracious God and merciful, slow to anger and of great kindness and repentedst Thee of the evil; and as I knew this "therefore I fled before into Tarshish" and I trusted in Thy mercy and patience that Thou wouldst pardon my transgression and not punish me. Therefore now, my Lord, take my life from me, I beseech Thee; for it is better for me to die than to live; because Thou hast repented of the evil of which Thou spakest to the wicked men of Nineveh, whose repentance was only for their own sake, and Thou hast brought me, Thy servant, to them—and now they look upon me as a liar, so that I would rather die than live'. And God confirmed this argument, as it says 'Then said the Lord: Thou doest well (*hahetev*) to be angry'. God told him that he was right to be angry. The *ha* in *hahetev* is not the *he* of questioning, but is the declarative *he*. If it had been interrogative, Jonah would have answered one way or another, as he does in a subsequent verse.

God revealed to Jonah by His holy Spirit why He had repented of the evil proclaimed against Nineveh, just as it says (Amos iii. 7): 'Surely the Lord God will do nothing, but He revealeth His secret to His servants, the prophets'. So it was revealed to Jonah at the very beginning of the forty days that he had proclaimed to Nineveh and he was very angry and tried to plead with God. But since God said 'Thou doest well to be angry', Jonah was appeased, because God agreed with him, and he was still hoping that the prophecy would be fulfilled. Hence it says 'So Jonah left the city and sat on the east-side (*mi-kedem*) of the city'. He left the sorrow he felt in his heart because of the city, but the city remained in the place of its wickedness, where it had formerly been (*mi-kedem*). 'And there made him a booth and sat under it in the shadow', i.e., his confidence and trust in God were like a booth. 'He sat under it in the shadow'—he withdrew himself under it in the shadow of his hope until he should see the fate of the city, whether or not it would be rescued from its doom at the conclusion of the forty days, which he had prophesied.

When God saw what Jonah was thinking, He revealed to him the secret and showed that what he thought was not good and could not be fulfilled. He provided illustrations by way of parable, as it says 'The Lord God prepared a gourd and let it come up over Jonah, that it might be a shadow over his head to deliver him from his grief; so Jonah was exceedingly glad of the gourd'. It says 'The Lord God prepared' using both Divine names because the growth of the gourd resembled that of the trees in the Garden of Eden, of which it is said' (Genesis ii. 9): 'Out of the ground made the Lord God to grow every tree that is pleasant to the sight'. Just as these trees were fully grown on the day of their creation, so was the gourd which came immediately up over Jonah. And just as these trees were specially delightful to behold, so was the gourd. It says 'To come up over Jonah that it might be a shadow over his head', i.e., a shadow for him in the event that the shadow of the booth under which he was sitting should pass away. And it says 'to deliver him from his grief'; should the shadow of the booth move, then the shadow of the gourd would protect him from the fierce heat. So Jonah was very glad on two counts—because of the beauty of the gourd and the benefit of the shade. This joy is like that of a man for this-worldly possessions, which have no permanence and are not causes for rejoicing on their acquisition nor for regret on their loss.

Because of his joy in things of this world, the Bible goes on to show how little is their worth and how insignificant their power and says 'God prepared a worm, when the morning arose the next day, and it smote the gourd, that it withered'. This worm is a metaphor for the days and nights that continually eat up the life of living things and they lose their days but do not realize it until their time comes. It says 'when the morning arose the next day' to show that it occurred at the appropriate time. The worm was destined to smite the gourd in the morning, because that is near the time when men need shade, i.e., when the sun shines strongly.

It continues 'It came to pass when the sun did arise' when shadow benefits man—'that God prepared an east wind at the ploughing time'—the time of the east wind. 'Ploughing time' implies a wind which ploughed up the land and brought dust and sand to Jonah's nostrils and moved his booth and its shadow away from him. 'The sun beat upon the head of Jonah that he was alarmed (va-yitallaf)' (from the same root as ullfu in Isaiah li. 20). He was amazed and disturbed that the gourd had withered and the booth afforded no shadow, and it says 'He wished in himself to die and said "it is better for me to die than to live" '; it is customary for those who are in trouble to despise their life and curse their days as Job said (iii. 11): 'Why did I not die from the womb? Why did I not give up the ghost when I came out of the belly?'

When God saw his sorrow and anger, He enquired as to the cause, as it says 'God said to Jonah "Doest thou well (*hahetev*) to be angry for the gourd"?' Here the *ha* in *hahetev* is the interrogative *he* and not the declarative *he* which was in the first verse, and here Jonah answered Him saying 'I am greatly angry, even unto death'. In this section, God is referred to as *elohim*, His name when He sits on the throne of judgment, as it says, 'God prepared a worm', 'God prepared an east wind', 'God said to Jonah', because Jonah was seeking judgment on account of the sorrow he felt. But when God told him of the verdict, which was dependent on the attribute of mercy, He is called 'the Lord' which is His name when He sits on the throne of mercy; as it says 'Then said the Lord: thou hast pity on the gourd for which thou hast not laboured neither madest it grow; which came up in a night and perished in a night'.

He said to him: 'You have had pity on the gourd because you thought it would give you pleasure, but you have not worked for it nor made it grow—it was an accident in the world, coming up in a night and perishing in a night, having neither profit nor permanence. And should I not have pity on Nineveh, that great city, wherein are more than sixscore thousand persons that cannot discern between their right hand and their left hand, and also much cattle'. Should not I, who want to establish this world on truth and to remove violence and iniquity, not for anything dependent on My glory, but because of My great mercy, spare that great city Nineveh wherein are more than sixscore thousand persons that cannot discern between their right hand and their left hand—i.e., they are not liable to punishment, because they have no conception of innocence or guilt. Moreover there is in it 'much cattle' which would all perish on account of the wickedness of the men of Nineveh. In view of their rejection of the evil which was causing them, their children and beasts to perish, do not mercy and justice require that I should have pity on the children and beasts and give life to the wicked along with them? The wicked will live on account of the children and beasts, instead of the children and beasts dying on their account'. When Jonah heard this just reasoning, he was satisfied and understood; he was silent and acknowledged its justice.

This prophecy clarifies the three grades of repentance and the differences between them. The reward of the first type is eternal life and endless peace; for the second, forgiveness and atonement with hope for the latter days; for the third, cancellation of the evil decree at the day of reckoning. For God is patient with the wicked in the hope that they will repent and so that they will have no cause for complaint when He punishes them on the day of reckoning. Each one of these three at the beginning acquires benefit—either really or apparently—the difference being in the latter days, when some of them are surrounded by kindness and others stand in great dread and fear. To enquire into those latter days, I return now to my main theme which I will start with the help of Him Who starts and concludes, may His name be praised and exalted for ever and ever unto all eternity.

PART FOUR

The passing-away of man and the latter end of the world

IT SAYS (Jeremiah i. 12): 'Then said the Lord unto me: Thou hast well seen; for I will watch over My word to perform it'. And also (Isaiah lv. 11): 'So shall My word be that goeth forth out of My mouth; it shall not return unto Me void, but it shall accomplish that which I please and it shall prosper in the thing whereto I sent it'. The former verse states that God carefully fulfils His words, whether they are for good or for evil. The latter verse says 'It shall not return unto Me void, but it shall accomplish that which I please' and we know that what He pleases is only for good, as it says (Jeremiah ix. 24): 'For I am the Lord who doeth lovingkindness, judgment and righteousness in the earth; for in these I delight, saith the Lord', i.e., I delight in these three things and in nothing else. These three are the basis of the world and they contain no evil.

At first sight, a comparison of these two verses presents a contradiction. It can be said that God's words contain harsh decrees and evil curses for the world—and the first verse states that He meticulously performs His words, which include curses and evils. It follows then that He performs the evil. The second verse states that He performs kindness, judgment and righteousness— these three alone and nothing bad (as compared with the first verse, according to which He performs curses and evils). We can say that those evils are not bad, but this is a difficult explanation for some people; or we can say that the two verses are contradictory and this is difficult for everybody. There are various answers to this problem.

(1) Some say that the statement 'But it shall accomplish that which I please' refers to 'the word that goeth forth out of My mouth', as it says 'So shall My word be that goeth forth out of My mouth'. Whatever goes forth from His mouth confers kindness on those who fear Him and maintains the world according to His will. The only words that issue from His mouth are the good deeds and kindnesses which He promises to His servants, and they are already sealed (to be performed) when they issue from His mouth. On the other hand, the decrees warning the wicked do not issue sealed and ready for performance, but are conditional, and He watches over them to perform them, according to this condition. The good things are given unconditionally but the evils are decreed conditionally; if repentance follows, they are cancelled, but if not, they are fulfilled. This would provide a superficial explanation, but it leaves the objection that it makes a distinction between the words of God—some would be decreed conditionally and others unconditionally. Moreover, if the decrees for the wicked are annulled by their repentance, so there should be a possibility of the words for the righteous being annulled, should they turn from their righteousness. So that is not a satisfactory answer and the problem remains.

(2) Others have answered the problem differently, saying that all events in the world can be divided into the good and the bad. The good is what benefits a man and has form and permanence, while the bad is the opposite. For example, life, which benefits the living, is to his benefit and has permanence, is good; whereas death, which annuls the benefit and brings in its place nothing of form or permanence (for the dead does not acquire anything in place of the life he has lost) is bad. Similarly as regards the one who hears and the one who is deaf; the one who sees and the one who is blind; the one who is clothed and the one who is naked; and other pairs, which can be classed together with one thing replacing the other—the one having form and called good, the other lacking form or benefit and called evil. Evil is the loss and absence of the

118

first and has itself no form or permanence. Those who hold this view say that God does good and grants His benefits to him who is worthy for a specific period, and at the end of that time they are separated from him. So that God does not decree that evil should come, but that the good should be removed, and evil occurs after the separation of the good. The evil confers nothing new on the thing from which the new form has been removed; this returns to the form it originally possessed before it received the good. So it can be said that the good is the action of God having form and permanence, and can be called an action, whereas its opposite, viz., evil—is not an act of God, as it is not an actual deed but is the negation of action—a non-action.

These people maintain that only good emanates from God and they interpret the verse (Isaiah lv. 11) 'So shall My word be that goeth forth out of My mouth', as referring to the good which He decrees—that it should not return until its mission is accomplished and His will has been done. The second verse 'For I will watch over My word to perform it' (Jeremiah i. 12)—they interpret as: He watches over the good, so that it will endure; and He is not concerned with the evil that comes after the separation of the good, because the good does not have to endure after the time decreed for it. They rely on the verse (Lamentations iii. 38) 'Out of the mouth of the All-High proceedeth not evil and good', i.e., both of them do not emanate from His mouth, but only good, and they explain the verse literally. However, this verse should not be explained literally, but, on the contrary, it shows how wrong is a person who thinks this way, as it says previously (Lamentations iii. 36): 'To subvert a man in his cause, the Lord seeth not'— the subversion a man speaks in his cause is that he says that the Lord does not see. The verse rebukes him, saying (ibid., 37) 'Who is he that saith and it cometh to pass when the Lord commandeth it not?' who is he who says that there is anything in actuality that has not been commanded by God? He then adds an interrogative rebuke, saying 'Out of the mouth of the All-High proceedeth not evil and good?', i.e., will it not proceed out of His mouth? Everything proceeds from Him and is established by His Divine word.

After rebuking him, it proceeds to explain the correct path, beginning with that leading to salvation, saying (ibid., 39–40) 'Wherefore doth a living man complain, a man for the punishment of his sins. Let us search and try our ways and turn again to the Lord'. It says 'living man' because a man who is alive can be guilty and still repent, but after his death he cannot repent. As our sages have said (*Avot* iv. 29) 'Let not thy imagination give thee hope that the grave will be a place of refuge for thee' to escape from what has been decreed concerning you, for the decrees of the world to come are not conditional like those of this world which can be mitigated or abolished as a result of repentance.

Do not think that you can repent after death; even a thousand repentances in the world to come for all the evil deeds committed in this world would be of no avail. 'For a living dog is better than a dead lion. For the living know that they shall die but the dead do not know anything' (Ecclesiastes ix. 4–5). The living knows what lies before him and can choose the good path, whereas the dead has only the one path, which he cannot know nor examine. So anyone, who imagines that after his death the deeds or prayers of his sons or members of his people can benefit him, is, according to all the sages, hoping in vain. Neither the Bible nor the sages make any such reference; but they mention the righteousness of the righteous and the wickedness of the wicked which can benefit or harm their sons after them, as it says (Jeremiah xxxii. 18): 'And recompensest the iniquity of the fathers into the bosom of their children after them' and (Exodus xx. 6) 'And showing mercy unto thousands of them who love Me and keep My commandments'. There is no place in the Torah from which it can be deduced that an action of a person in this world can benefit the dead—with one exception indicated by reason and attested to by the Torah. This is the case of the stolen object, not returned by a man before his death and for which he will be punished in the world to come. If this object is restored to its owners after the man's death, his punishment would be averted in the world to come, provided he had repented in his lifetime. According to the sages, there is one thing which can bring merit, namely, the teaching of Torah in this world; it will bring merit—even after his death—to the one who has taught, provided that, due to him, it continues to be studied.

(3) To return to the main subject: for the reason mentioned and similar considerations, the second reply does not answer the question with which we opened concerning the contradiction between the two verses. The proper answer is that it is God who does good and evil, everything and its opposite, and all originates from His will and His word, as it says (Jeremiah ix. 24): 'For I am the Lord who doeth kindness, judgment and righteousness'. This kindness is the goodness, kingship, wealth, grace and pleasantness He bestows on the inhabitants of this world through the attribute of kindness and truth—not because they are worthy but because His kindness and His praise fill all the world, as it says (Psalms xxxiii. 5) 'The earth is full of the kindness of the Lord'. It was with this praiseworthy attribute of kindness that He created the world and brought it from potentiality to actuality—not because the world had to be actualized or even understood the difference between potentiality and actuality, but so that He could extend His great kindness to all His creatures and to demonstrate His wisdom and great power in bringing out to actuality all that wisdom advised Him to bring out, and make it exist through the attribute of kindness; as it says (Psalms lxxix. 3) 'Kindness shall be built up for ever; Thy faithfulness shalt Thou establish in the very heaven'. The world was built up because of His kindness and not because mundane things had to go out to actuality and the world of change—but as they were long standing in potentiality and it was for their benefit, God brought them out to actuality, against their will, to fulfil the advice of His wisdom. Similarly, He has established the heavens by His faithfulness, i.e., the heavens were only forced to go out to actuality by the Creator of the World in order to improve the nature of the creatures of the earth which are subject to change and in order to establish a boundary beyond which they could not pass. This is the attribute of kindness ascribed to His glory.

The attribute of charity is the reward of the world to come, which is stored up for the righteous. It is called charity, which implies a gift to the deserving poor, for all those who die and leave the world—whether the pious righteous, believers in the middle category, and how much more the sinners and transgressors—must find mercy before God in order to find rest in the world to come. For only one in a thousand is worthy of reward in the world to come and that is the one whose merits exceed his faults. Those, whose merits and faults are equally balanced, should be satisfied to escape punishment—but God in His mercy and charity prescribes them a surfeit of merit and enables them to find rest. The merit of most people is infinitesimal when compared with their iniquities, but if they believe in the Torah, God in His mercy is generous in His judgment and forgives them, although they do not deserve reward and rest. This is the attribute of charity.

The attribute of justice is expressed in the equitable distribution of good and evil in the world—everyone of the righteous receiving his proper due, and each of the wicked according to what God deems fit. He grants goodness, joy and tranquillity to the righteous in the world to come, letting them find ease and rest to their hearts' content; as it says (Psalm cxlv. 19): 'He will fulfil the desire of them that fear Him'. In this world, He gives them trouble and distress in order to test them and so as ultimately to double their reward as it says (Deuteronomy viii. 2): 'To humble thee and to prove thee'—that it will ultimately be better for you. On the wicked, He decrees and seals evil and punishment in this world, so as to punish them and cut off all remembrance of them, as it says (Psalm xxxiv. 17): 'The face of God is against them that do evil to cut off the remembrance of them from the earth'. He gives the wicked good things, riches and possessions in this world that they should have no excuses nor claims in the world to come as it says (Deuteronomy vii. 10): 'And repayeth them that hate Him to their face to destroy them' and also (Psalms xcii. 8): 'When the wicked spring as the grass and when all the workers of iniquity do flourish—it is that they shall be destroyed for ever'.

Evil comes to the world in two ways. It either comes on the wicked to requite them for their actions or it comes on the righteous to test them and to correct them, so as ultimately to increase their reward, as in the case of Job, where it is said (Job xlii. 10): 'The Lord gave Job twice as much as he had before'.

122

Because Job's three friends did not understand this properly, they thought that evil comes to the world only as a punishment and did not realize that it can also come to the righteous to test them. Hence they accused Job and stated that the punishment that had befallen him must be the result of his evil deeds and the multitude of his iniquities; as Eliphaz the Temanite said to him (Job xxii. 5): 'Is not thy wickedness great and thy iniquities infinite?' and also (Job iv. 7): 'Remember I pray thee whoever perished being innocent, or where were the righteous cut off?' They brought proof to back their contentions, such as (Job viii. 3) 'Doth God pervert judgment or doth the Almighty pervert righteousness?' Obviously God does not pervert judgment, but He establishes judgment, so as to test the righteous man in order to increase his rewards and silence the wicked, so that they will have no excuses. Therefore Job was annoyed by their words, because in his heart he knew the bitterness of his spirit. Scripture attests to his righteousness when it says (Job i. 1) 'That man was perfect and upright and one that feared God and eschewed evil' and God tested him as He tests all the God-fearing. Because the friends of Job did not understand the significance of the punishments which befall the God-fearing, they accused Job—but he was guiltless. Hence God was displeased with their behaviour and was angry with them and rebuked them, as it says (Job xlii. 7): 'The Lord said to Eliphaz the Temanite: "My wrath is kindled against thee and against thy two friends, for ye have not spoken of Me the thing that is right as my servant Job has"'. For this iniquity, they should have been punished with all the punishments of Job to test them, just as the Lord had tested Job, but in His mercy He advised them to seek Job's forgiveness and ask him to pray for them. So, on Job's prayer, God forgave them, as it says (Job xlii. 8): 'Therefore take unto you now seven bullocks and seven rams and go to my servant Job', i.e., seek forgiveness from him; 'And offer up for yourselves a burnt offering' if he forgives you and prays for you; 'for him will I accept'; as he accepts you—'that I deal with you after your folly' not to test you with all the trials I brought on him. We see from here that one who suspects an upright person is like a lying witness and should be punished. And in his punishment he is liable to request forgiveness from the one he has suspected. Had the friends of Job not sought his forgiveness, God would not have forgiven them, and they would have been greatly punished, as it is written 'For them will I not accept'.

To return to the main subject: It is clear that the two verses quoted at the outset have identical implications—that good and evil are both decreed by God and came to the world by His word and will. God is always called by the name appropriate for bringing this attribute to bear upon man. Thus, for the good things of the world He is called merciful, compassionate, long-suffering and rewarding kindness and so on; for the evils He decrees on the world, He is called jealous, revengeful, wrathful and so on. This can be discerned from the example of Nineveh; when Jonah was seeking judgment from God, he says (Jonah iv. 2): 'For I know that Thou art a gracious God and merciful, slow to anger and of great kindness and repentest Thee of evil'. With all these good attributes, He was patient with the men of Nineveh. With the attribute of mercy, He sent Jonah to warn them in the hope that they would repent and the punishment would be annulled; with His attribute of patience, he granted a forty days' respite for repentance; and with His attribute of kindness, He accepted their repentance even though it was not for the sake of heaven. It says 'And repentest Thee of the evil'—with all these attributes, He repents of the evil, as it says (Exodus xxxii. 14): 'The Lord repented of the evil which He said He would do to His people.'

When it explains His vengeance in the Book of Nahum, it says first (Nahum i. 2): 'God is jealous and the Lord revengeth; the Lord revengeth and is furious; the Lord will take vengeance on His adversaries and He reserveth wrath for His enemies'. First He is called jealous and revengeful—attributes ascribed to His glory by which He decrees vengeance on the wicked out of His jealousy for their evil acts. Next it says 'The Lord revengeth and is furious' for He takes vengeance against those with whom He is angry on account of their evil deeds. It says 'The Lord will take vengeance on His adversaries'—on those who persist in their evil and do not repent. 'He reserveth wrath for His enemies' who abandon their wickedness, but not for the sake of heaven. God is patient with them initially because of their repentance but their wickedness is remembered again on the day of reckoning as was the case with the men of Nineveh, with whom He was patient and refrained from executing the evil that had been decreed against them—but it was stored up before Him, as it says 'The Lord is slow to anger and great in power and will not at all acquit the wicked'. This mentions the two attributes which caused the evil to be annulled from Nineveh—namely, His kindness and His patience—but He did not forgive them completely, because their repentance was imperfect; He held them guiltless initially, but not so ultimately, as it says 'And will not at all hold guiltless the wicked'.

God watches over the evil—to bring it on the wicked. And even if He is patient with them, He does not forgive them entirely, but eventually exacts their punishment, as it says (Psalms v. 5): 'For Thou art not a God that hath pleasure in wickedness; neither shall evil dwell with Thee. The foolish shall not stand in Thy sight; Thou hatest all workers of iniquity. Thou shalt destroy them that speak lies; the Lord will abhor the bloody and deceitful man'. First, it mentions what is displeasing to God and divides it into two categories—wickedness and evil. Wickedness is by deed and word of mouth and evil is in the heart. Those two categories incorporate all types of abomination hated by God and they will not exist in this world, as it says 'neither shall evil dwell with Thee'—it will not dwell in Thy world.

Wickedness and evil come to the world in two ways: (1) intentionally or deceitfully, when the person acts evilly despite understanding the glory of God; or (2) through folly or ignorance, when the persons act without knowing the glory of God. To God both are equally culpable, because there is no distinction between the consequences of their actions, and He seeks to end evil in this world, whether it is caused intentionally or unintentionally. That is why it returns to the subject and says 'the foolish shall not stand in Thy sight', i.e., all who act evilly—even if out of madness and without intention—will not stand in His sight because God hates all who do evil. It continues by explaining how it will be that they will not dwell in His world or stand in His sight, saying, that He causes them to perish—'Thou shalt destroy them that speak lies'. It calls them lies because to God no iniquity is greater than lying which is as grave as murdering, as it says at the end of the section 'The Lord will abhor the bloody and deceitful man'.

From all that we have said, we can conclude and believe that God will cut off all the wicked nations from the earth, as it says (Zephaniah iii. 6): 'I have cut off the nations, their cities are destroyed; their towers are desolate; I made their streets waste so that no man passeth by; there is no man, there is no inhabitant'. God cuts them off, makes waste their dwellings and depopulates their cities. Another verse says (Isaiah xxxiii. 12): 'The people shall be as the burnings of lime; as thorns cut up shall they be burned in the fire' showing that once they are cut off, they have no existence just as thorns burnt in the fire cease to exist. The verse adds a further explanation, classing together all the nations which will be destroyed, saying (Isaiah x. 23): 'For the Lord God of hosts shall make a consumption even determined in the midst of all the land'. He will destroy the wicked of the world and cut off them and their seed.

It says 'in the midst of all the land' and not 'in the midst of all the nations', so that it should not be thought to refer solely to the wicked among men. It shows that He removes all evil qualities and enmity from animals and beasts as He does from man, as it says (Isaiah xi. 7): 'The cow and the bear shall feed; their young ones shall lie down together; and the lion shall eat hay with the ox'. At that time all the wicked destined for destruction shall perish, most of the nations of the world will be lost entirely and only the righteous of God's people will remain together with other nations who believe in the Torah. He will also bring trials to His people to test them, as it says (Zechariah xiii. 9): 'And will refine them as silver is refined and will try them as gold is tried', because His will is to refine them so as to remove all dross and blemish, as it says (Isaiah i. 25): 'And I will turn My hand upon thee and purge away thy dross and take away all thy tin' and subsequently it says 'I will restore thy judges as at the first'.

Thus you understand that at that time God will make a distinction between Israel and the other nations of the world. It says about the nations (Isaiah xxviii. 22): 'Now therefore be ye not mockers, lest your bones be made strong; for I have heard from the Lord God of hosts a consumption even determined upon the whole earth'. He brings the nations to an end and causes them to perish, but in His mercy He spares a goodly remnant of His people, as it says (Jeremiah xxx. 11): 'Though I made a full end of all the nations here . . . yet will I not make a full end of thee . . .' And it says (Nahum i. 9): 'What do ye imagine against the Lord? He will make an utter end; affliction shall not rise up the second time'. It says: 'Affliction shall not rise up the second time' for all the troubles He brings upon His people, for which He exacts vengeance from the other nations. He tests His people at that time, so as to remove from their midst any heretic who lacks faith, to pardon the sins of the sinners, and to strengthen the faith of the waverers. As it says (Daniel xi. 35): 'Some of them of understanding shall stumble to try ("clarify") them and to purge and to cleanse them even to the time of the end'; some of them of understanding shall stumble in the iniquity of the wicked, who lead them to sin. This verse can be explained in two ways:

(1) Those of understanding stumble, i.e., they stumble in iniquity, in that they did not warn the rest of the people and lead them in the right path and correct them with words of Torah, so that they would return to God and be saved from the punishment decreed for them. Hence those of understanding stumble together with them. It mentions only those of understanding, because they will eventually be purged and cleansed, for they are able to undergo the purging. But the rest of the people, who lack understanding, will not have the strength to be purged, much less be fully cleansed.

(2) Others say that this verse speaks of the period of the Exile. 'Those of understanding' refers to the men of the Great Assembly and the other scholars who were dispersed by Titus in various countries. In this connection 'stumbles in iniquity' refers to the leaders and Sadducees, etc., who caused this Exile. It says 'to purge them', meaning their exile from Palestine, and 'to clarify' through the long days of the Exile, which are a period of purging, as it says (Isaiah lxi. 9): 'All that see them shall acknowledge them,

that they are the seed which the Lord hath blessed'. It says 'to cleanse' about the days of salvation, when they will be cleansed and purified from all blemish. It puts these trials in proper order, as it says 'to refine them and to purge and to cleanse them' which is the order of gold or silver refinement—first they are poured out and refined, then the refiner sifts them and separates them from the tin or lead or other metals until they are whitened and cleansed from any dross. So God tries His people and tests them so as to remove any guilt or iniquity until those who are left are pure and smelted like gold, which has been smelted seven times. Thus it says (Nahum ii. 1) 'Behold upon the mountains the feet of him that bringeth good tidings that publisheth peace; O Judah, keep thy solemn feasts, perform thy vows; for the wicked shall no more pass through thee; he is utterly cut off'. Every evil man shall be cut off from his people and from the world at the time of salvation, as it says 'Behold upon the mountain the feet of him that bringeth good tidings' and 'good tidings' mean tidings of salvation. So it says previously 'to refine them and to purge and cleanse them even to the time of the end', i.e., the refinement and the subsequent processes will last until the time of final salvation.

In and around the time of salvation, grave troubles will fall upon Israel, as it says (Daniel xii. 1): 'At that time shall Michael, the great prince, stand up . . . and there will be a time of trouble such as never was, since there was a nation even to that same time . . . and at that time thy people shall be delivered, everyone that shall be found written in the book'. All who fear heaven should be watchful for that time and should mend his ways and correct his deeds and not make his heart more evil by saying that we will never witness such a period, or that however we act, we will be inscribed in the Book thanks to the merits of our ancestors. These are vain comforts and words of laziness and weakness. A person should also not be overwhelmed by trouble and tribulations for his iniquities, saying 'What can I do, for my iniquities are so great? How can there be a remedy?' but let him concentrate on what can heal his trouble, and he will understand that the doors of penitence are open wide and those who follow this path prosper—

and if he hastens to repent, he will be worthy of being inscribed in the Book.

Now we will consider these verses and the merit to which they refer. First we say that they refer to the perfectly righteous for whose sake the world was established, as is said of them (Isaiah lvii. 15): 'I dwell in the high and holy place with him also that is of a contrite and humble spirit to revive the spirit of the humble and to revive the heart of the contrite ones'. God brings His Torah to the dwellings of the humble and the contrite to revive the spirit of these two categories; these and those like them are the ones inscribed in the Book, and their qualities and deeds should now be examined.

First we bring proof from the Bible, and to explain this properly we say that all who believe in God and worship him, can be divided by their habits into three categories:

(1) The first group does not participate at all in the events of this world or even think of them. They are sep. ated all their days to serve God and heaven. They can be one or many but they are reckoned as a single individual, because they are indistinguishable in their qualities and their separation from all occupation. This man is called 'separated for God' or 'devoted to God'.

(2) The second group toils in the affairs of this world and participates in its events, but at the same time observes all the commandments. These cannot be classified as a single individual, because all the inhabitants of this world must participate in its affairs and help one another, so there are many of them helping each other—but not one seeks more than he requires and none cheats his neighbour or is suspicious of another man, and there is no rivalry or strife. We call these men 'a family', 'a righteous community' or a 'faithful city'.

(3) The third division resembles the second in most of its actions, but is suspicious of others and is on guard against its enemies—and therefore appoints a king to rule and have power over it and lead it on the right way, correcting all who deviate from it. It goes to war with its enemies and is occupied solely with what is for its benefit. This division is called a 'just kingdom', 'a righteous nation' or 'an established province'.

These are the three divisions of believers—there are neither more nor less. Corresponding to them and in addition to them are many divisions of the wicked and transgressors who have no portion amongst the God-fearing, but we are not going to investigate them.

Returning to our main theme, we say that God has divided His holy Torah for the three above-mentioned divisions of believers, showing each the proper way and statutes, so that each should firmly adhere to the proper way and not be deflected or heed anything else. The basis of His Torah, which He commanded His people, is the Ten Commandments. These incorporate all the commandments and statutes which a man must do including the general principles which are sufficient for the first group, the individual separated for God. He requires no further explanation and these earn him the life of the world to come.

To clarify this subject properly, I want to explain this entire section. All man's actions in this world fall under three headings:

(a) Relations between man and God.

(b) Relations between man and his household.

(c) Relations between man and the rest of mankind.

Each one of these can be subdivided into commandments connected with thought, commandments connected with speech, and commandments accompanied by actions. If you work this out completely, you will see that there are nine commandments covering all aspects of human conduct which are required to rectify the world. This rectification can be divided into two aspects:

(a) It can be attained through human knowledge and thoughts and by erecting fences and limitations to restrict the activities of men in this world, as in all human legislation which corrects deeds and affairs in this world but is not intended for the world to come, according to the sages.

(b) The second aspect is not rectified by human actions or thoughts, nor is it founded on man's faulty knowledge, but it springs from the fount of all wisdom—from the mouth of God. It leads to benefit in this world and the world to come.

130

Certainly the rectification is divisible into the nine above-mentioned divisions, neither more nor less. But we must make known their source and this provides us with a tenth division. The tenth is the most important and all the others are dependent upon it. So we have a total of ten sayings obtained by logical deduction. Those ten comprise all the 613 commandments listed in the Torah, but were first incorporated in the Ten Commandments, which are adequate for the truly God-fearing and those who are separated unto God. Subsequently they are explained and clarified two or three times to warn the rest of the people and show them how to behave. We will explain how these ten include all the commandments and how they suffice for every God-fearing man who is removed from this world and separated unto God.

The first commandment shows that the other nine emanate from God, and that all His commandments and advice should be observed. The next three explain commandments between God and man. The first teaches the nature of proper faith, which depends on the heart, and it covers all those commandments dependent on the worship, love and fear of God. The second explains faith, expressed through speech, viz., oaths, vows, mentioning the names of other gods and similar commandments. The third commandment explains faith dependent on action, including Sabbaths, festivals, New Moons, etc. Those three commandments deal with matters between man and God.

The next three are concerned with relations between man and his household. Precedence is taken by the first, commanding the honour of one's parents. This depends on the heart because honour which does not emanate from the heart is not real honour (kavod) but a difficulty (koved) or nuisance. This command covers not only honour of parents, but honour of all who study the Torah and all who are God-fearing. The second is 'Thou shalt not murder', i.e., killing a person or anything similar. It is incorporated in this section of commandments between man and his household, although the warning is against killing anyone—but in particular one is warned against harming his household and his friends. And since the verse warns against harming generally, we understand that it refers to everyone else, together with one's household. The

131

third commandment, depending on action, is 'Thou shalt not commit adultery', and that includes all commandments against lewdness, obscenity, etc. This obviously belongs in the division of relations between man and his household.

There remains the final division—relations between man and the rest of mankind, and these are dealt with in the last three commandments. The first is 'Thou shalt not steal' which covers stealing, robbery, things taken by violence, and any such action between man and his fellows not belonging to his household—as stealing, etc., does not depend on the action of a man with his own house and property. This section first gives the commandments connected with practical action because they are the most serious in relations between man and his fellow-men, unlike the relations between man and God where the most serious commandments depend on the heart. The second commandment in this section is 'Thou shalt not bear false witness', which covers all commandments depending on speech between man and his fellow, including false witnesses, slander, etc. The third commandment is 'Thou shalt not covet' which covers all commandments connected with impure thought between a man and his fellow, such as desire, revenge, grudge-bearing, causeless hatred, etc., as the sages have explained in their writings and there is no need for me to expound here.

The Ten Commandments incorporate all the positive and negative commandments mentioned in the Torah. They are written in the singular, because they are a general rule given by God to Moses on Mount Sinai for his conduct and for all the separated individuals who would come after him and want to follow His ways with all their heart. The Bible does not have to command and warn them in the plural, because all the separated individuals are united in their heart and are regarded as a single individual, without distinction in their devotion even though they are distinguished in honour and superiority.

Of all the Ten Commandments, two are in the form of positive commands. One is 'Remember the Sabbath day', which is a command to rest from work, as these individuals have no interest in the work of this world and labour only in the work of heaven, and they are separated from all this-worldly pleasures. The second one is 'Honour thy father' referring to one's father and mother who have given him life in this world, and connected with this is honouring the Torah, those who teach it, and those who study it who bring him life in the world to come. Seven of the commandments are negative commandments, because these separate individuals have at no time any interest in this-worldly occupations. You should not be concerned by the fact that the general rule shows that they do not fulfil the Biblical commandment of being fruitful and multiplying which was the first of the commandments given to Adam; remember the words of Ben Azzai that the world can be established by others.[1] You should know that the words of Ben Azzai are the words of the separated individual. Thus Moses, the first deserving to be called by this name and the first to receive the Ten Commandments, was separated from women from the time he received the commandments. Most of the prophets mentioned in the Bible acted similarly, as we find no mention of their having had children. This was not true of all the separated individuals, e.g., Samuel whose sons are mentioned by name, but it is proper conduct for the separated individuals not to indulge in marital intercourse except for the purpose of procreation and not for pleasure or lust. These are the characteristics of those who are separated for God.

In concluding our discussion of that great category of individuals, we say that God gave the Torah to Israel so that with it they should inherit two worlds: success and long life in this world, eternal life and reward in the world to come. These two merits are acquired by the Ten Commandments. Reward in the world to come is acquired by the first four Commandments, and, to be more precise, by the first Commandment concerning the unity of God; for belief in the unity of God and His choice of His people Israel and His honouring them with His Torah—which is the meaning of the first commandment—will suffice to acquire the reward of the life of the world to come and no further actions are required; for the following three commandments, which make one worthy of the world to come, are not actions, but warnings

[1] *Yevamot* 63b.

against actions, being the negative commands 'Thou shalt have no ...' 'Thou shalt not do ...' 'Thou shalt not take ...' Even the fourth commandment which is put positively, carries the negative prohibition of 'Thou shalt do no work' ... (Exodus xx. 10).

Man, therefore, acquires the life of the world to come by complete belief in God and His Torah and labouring solely for the sake of heaven, and in this way nothing harms him in this world. But prosperity in this world ensues from the observance of the remaining six commandments. Proof of this is contained in the punishment stipulated for transgressing the first four commandments, as it says (Exodus xx. 5): 'Visiting the iniquities of the fathers upon the children' and (ibid., 7): 'For the Lord will not hold him guiltless that taketh His name in vain'. But in the other six commandments it mentions the prosperity of this world, as it says: 'Honour thy father and thy mother that thy days may be lengthened', to show that if you carefully observe this and the subsequent commandments, your affairs will prosper and so will your life in this world—and if you observe them for the sake of heaven, your reward is increased in the world to come. But if you despise them and do not fulfil them properly, you lose the affairs of this world, but you do not forfeit a portion in the world to come, as long as you continue to believe in the first commandment. Proof of this is that our ancestors in First Temple times, even though they included idol-worshippers and were liable for exile, sword and famine etc., still did not lose the merits of their ancestors, because they did not deny the essence of the Torah and faith in God.

We see from this that a man in this world can reach the ranks of the separated individuals by keeping aloof from the affairs of this world and despising its evil desires, by refraining from any action not connected with the commandments and by rejecting worldly possessions and despising all wealth and riches; men like this can be confident that they will receive their reward in the world to come. Therefore our sages have said that God chose for His people Israel this attribute of poverty, so that they will be removed from this world and cleave to the world to come; happy is he whom God has rewarded so that he despises evil and chooses good.

To return to the main subject. As soon as the Ten Commandments had been decreed and Moses had been warned and shown the correct path, God appointed him as a faithful messenger to His people to show the correct path to the holy community or the faithful city, which we mentioned before. It is customary for a person who is appointed over a thing to be first warned about it and to be appointed in the course of this warning: thus it was in the case of Joshua. When God instructed Moses to appoint Joshua, He said (Numbers xxvii. 18–19): 'Take thee Joshua the son of Nun, a man in whom is spirit and lay thy hand upon him; and set him before Eleazar the priest and before all the congregation; and give him a charge in their sight;' i.e., just as in the sight of all Israel I gave you the Ten Commandments with which you were warned and then immediately appointed you My messenger, so you must give your commands to Joshua in the sight of all the congregation and by this act you will be appointing him, as it says (ibid., 20): 'And shalt put some of thine honour on him'.

Similarly we say here that when Moses was warned with the Ten Commandments, he was made a messenger to Israel to teach them the explanation of the general rules implicit in the Ten Commandments. He began with the first of the Commandments, with which he had been warned, namely 'Thou shalt have no other God'. God said to him 'I spoke to thee in the singular, but thou teach it to the children of Israel in the plural; I said "thou shalt have no other gods"—say to them (Exodus xx. 19) "Ye have seen that I have talked to you from heaven; you shall not make with me gods of silver neither shall ye make unto ye gods of gold"'. Just as the command 'Thou shalt not have . . .' was the first Commandment with which Moses was warned, so 'You shall not make with me gods of silver neither shall ye make gods of gold' was the first commandment Moses was instructed to teach the children of Israel. This provides strong proof that the Ten Commandments suffice for those who comprehend their general principles and appreciate how they should be divided—and these are the separated individuals.

It will also be clear that the commandments in the rest of the three books of the Pentateuch—Exodus, Leviticus and Numbers—are the statutes and judgments intended for the separate community. These commandments are all contained in the framework of the Ten Commandments and are all hidden there, but this meditation of the sad soul is not the appropriate place to discover how they are concealed there and how they should be explained; perhaps God will give me the privilege of explaining this properly elsewhere. Here we state that these three books explain the religion of the holy community, which does not occupy itself with this-worldly affairs more than is absolutely essential for the sake of its households and people, and it is oblivious of external events. The children of Israel conducted themselves according to these commandments and statutes during all the forty years they were in the wilderness, when they did not require any commandments beyond those expounded in those three books, because there was no need to be concerned with outside events, as they were protected and surrounded by a pillar of cloud.

These commandments and statutes are adequate for all the exiled communities of Israel throughout the world today. They cannot shut out external events nor can they prepare arms to repulse their enemies; and they must rely on the many mercies of God promised in the Torah, as it says (Leviticus xxvi. 44): 'Yet for all that they be in the land of their enemies, I will not reject them, nor will I abhor them; to destroy them and to break my covenant with them, for I am the Lord their God', i.e., the covenant I made to be their God, as it says (Leviticus xxii. 33): 'I am the Lord that brought you out of the land of Egypt to be your God; I am the Lord'. 'I am the Lord' here implies an oath. The sufferings mentioned in Leviticus xxvi. 3ff. refer to the Exile following the destruction of the Second Temple, in which we are now, and we trust in God's mercy to hasten our salvation; it does not speak of the exile following the destruction of the First Temple, as we will explain later.

After the explanation of the worship of the second of our three divisions—the holy community—we must consider the worship of the just kingdom, which has to take external events into

136

consideration and guard against those who provoke them. This division requires additional commandments and statutes and these are set forth in the Book of Deuteronomy. The only distinction between the second and the third division is that the latter has to take into account external events and has to interest itself in affairs of this world, and so requires fences and limits, not required by the second category. So we find that the commandments explained in Deuteronomy are the same as in the three previous books, but Deuteronomy adds fences and limits required for people who have to defend themselves from provocation. It also adds statutes and commandments connected with agricultural work and other occupations that may lead to dispute, and explains laws of fines, military disciplines, battle order and the rest of the commandments mentioned in Deuteronomy, but not in the rest of the Pentateuch because they are not necessary for the separate community which is not concerned with the affairs of this world. The generation of the wilderness had no need to be concerned with external events and their every requirement was provided by God—and that is why many commandments mentioned in Deuteronomy do not appear elsewhere in the Pentateuch, while many commandments appear in the earlier books that are not mentioned in Deuteronomy, i.e., those connected with the Temple service, which are relevant to all believers, whether or not they have to be concerned with this-worldly affairs.

There is one group of commandments concerning which the holy community is warned in one way, and the men of the faithful city in another way, viz., the commandments mentioned both in the earlier books and in Deuteronomy, but in different ways. To mention all the differences would mean prolonging the subject unnecessarily, but we will give a few useful examples, remembering our view that Deuteronomy contains legislation relevant to the conduct of the children of Israel after they entered the Land of Israel. As it says at the beginning of that section (Deuteronomy iv. 5): 'Behold, I have taught you statutes and judgments even as the Lord my God commanded me that ye should do so in the midst of the land whither ye go to possess it', i.e., the previous sections of the Pentateuch have explained how you should behave in the wilderness and now in the Book of Deuteronomy I will explain all that the Lord has commanded you to do in the Land of Israel. As it says (Deuteronomy xii. 9): 'For ye are not yet come to the rest and to the inheritance which the Lord your God giveth you'.

After this introduction, it gives the Ten Commandments in the singular in the same order as in the Book of Exodus—there is not a single difference in the first three commandments which constitute the foundation of faith, and are in themselves sufficient to acquire the life of the world to come, for those who believe in them and act accordingly. In the seven other commandments the language is changed, if necessary. In the fourth commandment, it substitutes 'Remember' for 'Observe', but we will not go into the reason for the change because it is not germane to our subject. And for the same reason we will not go into the details of all the other changes, but only those that are relevant. In the fourth command it makes an addition, saying 'Remember the Sabbath Day—as the Lord Thy God commanded thee' and in the fifth commandment 'Honour thy father—as the Lord thy God commanded thee' in order to inform you that these things, which would be right even if not commanded by the mouth of God, are here stressed as positive commands because there exists the possibility of differing degrees (in the performance of these two commandments).[1] And it makes no further reference to 'commanding' in the other five commandments, which are all negative, because in an action there can be a distinction between something done properly and something not done properly, between what is skilfully done and what is not skilfully done as well as other differences between one action and another; but there is no distinction to be drawn in the negation of an action.

In the fourth commandment, in the version of Deuteronomy, it makes the further addition of 'ox and ass' as it says 'Thou shalt do no work, thou and thy son and thy daughter and thy manservant and thy maidservant and thine ox and thine ass and all thine animals'. It does not mention 'ox and ass' in Exodus, because there it was speaking to the separate individuals who were not

[1] The text here is unclear.

138

occupied with sowing or ploughing—and God was feeding them from His heaven with manna. But in Deuteronomy it speaks about the separated community, which has to occupy itself with agriculture. This is also why it mentions 'field' in the tenth commandment of the Deuteronomy version as it says 'neither shalt thou desire thy neighbour's house, his field, his manservant or his maidservant' whereas in the Exodus version 'field' is not mentioned. We will not go into details of other differences, but what we have said is sufficient to show that Deuteronomy refers to the entire period of settlement during the kingdom, starting from the conquest under Joshua up to the First Temple Exile.

After concluding the teaching of the Ten Commandments to those who dwell in the Land of Israel, to show which legislation is relevant for them in order to establish justice and truth, it next teaches the laws concerning the king who would be ruling them and instructs them concerning wars they would have to fight against all who would provoke them. After this section, it concludes with a rebuke, explaining the Exile with which the First Kingdom ended; this is the rebuke contained in the section *Ki Tavo*. We state that this rebuke applies to this exile because it mentions all the troubles which fell upon our ancestors in that exile. For example, it says (Deuteronomy xxviii. 36): 'The Lord shall bring thee and thy king which thou shalt set over thee' these were the kings of Israel who were to be brought to exile—'to a nation which neither thou nor thy fathers have known', i.e., Halah and Havor, cities of Media which were neither mentioned nor heard of in all the Scriptures until that Exile. The kings of Israel were exiled to those places for they were not of the anointed according to the word of the Lord, as it says 'The king which thou shalt set over thee' not 'Thy king anointed by the word of the Lord'. At the conclusion of that rebuke it says (ibid., 68): 'And the Lord shall bring thee into Egypt again with ships'—this refers to those who remained in Jerusalem and were then brought into Egypt by ships after the murder of Gedaliah, as it says (II Kings xxv. 26): 'All the people both small and great and the captains of the armies arose and came to Egypt, for they were afraid of the Chaldees'. It continues 'There shall ye be sold unto your enemies for bondmen and bondwomen, and no man shall buy you'. You can apply to this what Esther said (Esther vii. 4): 'If we had been sold for bondmen and bondwomen, I had held my peace', i.e., if we had been sold for bondmen and bondwomen, I would have been silent and said that this had been decreed for us in this Exile; but now that I see we are sold for slaughter and destruction and I find no mention of slaughter in all the rebuke forecasting this Exile, I know that the wicked intends harming us, but that is not the harm decreed on us because of the king we elected to rule over us on account of whose transgressions the Exile was decreed; for it says (ibid.) 'For our affliction is not like the harm of a king'.

There is no mention at the end of the rebuke in Deuteronomy of any consolation, because the period of the First Exile and the Second Temple were reckoned by God as one period of rebuke or a long delay, as He says to Daniel (Daniel ix. 24) 'Seventy times seven are decreed upon thy people and upon thy holy city to restrain transgression and to make an end of sins', etc. Those 'seventy times seven' mentioned are the 490 years covering the period of the First Exile and the Second Temple. At the conclusion of that section, there is a hint of the Second Temple Exile, when it says (Daniel ix. 27): 'And half a seven he shall cause the sacrifices and the meal offerings to cease'—this 'half a seven' fulfils the seventy times seven from the destruction of the First Temple to the destruction of the Second Temple, which was followed by the Second Temple Exile, and so consolation is not mentioned in the rebukes of Deuteronomy. But it immediately gives a strong hint of consolation, saying (Deuteronomy xxix. 1): 'These are the words of the covenant which the Lord commanded Moses to make with the children of Israel', viz., when they come to the land for which He is laying down rules of conduct for them and that is apart from the covenant He made with them at Horeb, which mentions all the great consolation that will eventually come to them. The rebuke in the Torah contains a mention of the sword, which does not appear in Deuteronomy. In the First Exile Israel was saved through Divine mercy from all persecution, and 'being put to the sword'—but in the Second Exile, because of our great sins, there have been many persecutions and troubles and being put to the sword, as foretold in the earlier rebukes (Leviticus xxvi. 33) 'You will I scatter among the nations and I will draw out the sword after you'. He concludes this rebuke and punishments with the consolation of redemption (ibid., 44): 'Yet for all that when they be in the land of their enemies, I will not reject them neither will I abhor them'. And it says (ibid., 42): 'Then will I remember My covenant with Jacob . . . and I will remember my covenant with their ancestors, whom I brought forth out of the land of Egypt in the sight of the nations, that I might be their God; I am the Lord', i.e., I am the Lord who redeems you a second time in the sight of all the nations.

Thus the rebuke in Deuteronomy, without any doubt, indicates the First Temple Exile, and that in the earlier part of the Pentateuch refers to the Second Temple Exile. Every wise man should rejoice whenever he reads and repeats these rebukes, and thank God who has strengthened us to sustain the great troubles and rebukes; and we have not forgotten God nor forsaken His Torah. We trust implicitly that God, who has tried us with all those punishments according to His will, will fulfil the good things and consolations of which He has told us through His prophets. I am astonished at those people who are pained when they read these rebukes and rush their reading, as if they were something terrifying of which they were frightened. I find no sense in it, because we know that all the punishments mentioned have already befallen us and we have borne them with the mercy of God, and it is unusual for a person to be afraid of what is past as long as he is confident it will not recur—as we are; indeed it is customary for a man to be joyful for every good thing he anticipates in the future. So we should rejoice when we hear of the troubles that have already befallen us, because they strengthen our faith and make us confident that the consolation written after them will also come to pass. So in my view those people who are pained when they hear those rebukes are fools, and their faith in God is not very profound.

I return to the main subject. Because Moses concluded the rebuke in Deuteronomy without mention of consolation, he

subsequently returns to the subject, saying (Deuteronomy xxx. 1):
'And it shall come to pass when all these things are come upon
thee the blessing and the curse which I have set before thee'—
which I have set before thee now as well as previously in the
Pentateuch—'and thou shalt call them to mind among all the
nations whither the Lord thy God has driven thee'—i.e., in those
days, when you will no longer be separate from the nations, but
will be among them. It says (Deuteronomy xxx. 2): 'And shalt
return to the Lord thy God and shalt hearken to His voice . . .
then the Lord thy God will turn thy captivity and have compassion upon thee and will return and gather thee from all the
peoples'. Thus salvation will come immediately after the repentance of Israel in its exile, namely in their hearkening to the voice
of the Lord. It would seem at first sight that Israel in its exile had
not been hearkening to the voice of the Lord before their repentance, because it says 'And thou shalt hearken to the voice of the
Lord', i.e., to which you had not been hearkening. But it is
difficult for believers to say of all our sages and pious and upright
men who occupy themselves with the Torah in this Exile that
they do not hearken to the voice of the Lord, as this verse would
imply. So we should enquire into the nature of this 'voice', to
which the sages and the righteous have not hearkened throughout
the Exile; they have suffered its tribulations although maintain-
ing the Divine covenant.

To explain this, we say that the verb *shama* (hearken) in this
context can be interpreted in three ways in Hebrew:

(*a*) Hearing of the ear—which does not imply comprehension;
e.g. (Job. xlii. 5): 'I had heard of thee by the hearing of the ear';
(Genesis xiv. 14): 'And when Abram heard that his brother had
been taken captive'.

(*b*) Receiving advice or command; e.g. (Genesis xvi. 2): 'And
Abram hearkened to the voice of Sarah', or (Exodus iii. 18): 'And
they shall hearken unto him'.

(*c*) Understanding; e.g. (Isaiah xxxvi. 11): 'Speak, I pray Thee, to
Thy servants in the Aramean language, for we understand it';
(Genesis xli. 15): 'When thou hearest a dream, thou canst interpret
it', i.e., understand its interpretation.

Thus the verb *ve-shamata* in the verse 'And shalt return to the Lord thy God and shalt hearken to (*ve-shamata*) His voice' derives from the third meaning, understanding—and does not mean merely, as is its meaning in most places, passive hearing. It implies that you will understand His voice which you have heard from the midst of the fire; concerning this it says (Deuteronomy iv. 12): 'Ye heard the voice of the words, but you saw no form; only a voice', i.e., you merely heard the voice in its usual meaning, but got no mental picture and did not grasp its internal form nor anything apart from the sound.

The voice that issues from God comes to this world with one of two objects:

(*a*) To decree and realize God's words; e.g., 'God said "Let there be light" ' (Genesis i. 12) and the rest of the sayings by which the world was created; and

(*b*) To warn and command: e.g., God said to Adam: 'Of every tree of the garden thou mayest freely eat; but of the tree of knowledge of good and evil, thou shalt not eat of it' (Genesis ii. 16–17).

The 'hearing' of the Ten Commandments by Israel at Sinai had both implications—to be heard and to be performed. The implication of 'Thou shalt have no other gods before me' and the rest of the commandments was a warning and a command; Israel was to observe them accordingly from the time of revelation until the time of salvation. Consequently there were those who accepted and acted properly and there were those who did not act properly; hence there were the transgressors and the meritorious. God's ultimate intention was to decree and realize the commandments, so the meaning of 'Thou shalt not have other gods before Me' is that such a thing is eternally inconceivable—therefore, from the time of salvation, all Israel will have no alternative but to observe the entire Torah properly, and will have neither the possibility nor the ability to transgress as no created thing can transgress what has been irrevocably decreed for them. All Israel in those days will behave as the righteous separated unto God, whose conduct we have already explained. The verse clearly explains this when it says (Deuteronomy xxx. 6): 'The Lord thy God will circumcise

143

thy heart, and the heart of thy seed to love the Lord thy God with all thy heart and with all thy soul for the sake of thy life', because God removes the hardness and foreskin of your heart, which was preventing you from understanding the voice of the Lord, however interpreted to them, 'for the sake of thy life'— for the sake of the life in the world to come. Previously it says (Deuteronomy xi. 13): 'To love the Lord thy God and to serve Him with all thine heart and with all thy soul' and at the end of the section (Deuteronomy xi. 21) it says: 'That your days may be multiplied and the days of your children on the land', i.e., when you love God with all your heart and soul, because of His commandments and act in this world according to His will, He will make you prosper in this world, the original plan of which has been perverted by man's iniquities; and He makes it prosper and improve when man prospers and improves—and He changes it when man changes his ways. But when you love Me because of My decree and My word, the world prospers according to My original plan, not on account of human action, and the only reward of your love is the life of the world to come: therefore it says: 'for the sake of your life' and nothing else. The reward in the first verse alludes to the affairs of this world, as it says (Deuteronomy xi. 14): 'I will give you the rain of the land in its due season' and later (ibid., 21) 'that your days may be multiplied and the days of your children upon the Land that the Lord swore unto you'.

This subject is dealt with in the prophecy of Jeremiah who says (Jeremiah xxxi. 31): 'Behold the days come, saith the Lord, that I will make a new covenant with the House of Israel and the House of Judah' referring to the days of redemption, for whose early advent we hope, when all the exiles of Israel and Judah will be redeemed. And it says (ibid., 32): 'Not according to the covenant that I made with their fathers in the days when I took them by the hand to bring them out of the land of Egypt; forasmuch as they brake my covenant, although I was a Lord over them, saith the Lord'; i.e., they broke My covenant because, although I gave them the possibility of being God-fearing and performing good deeds, 'I was a Lord over them', as they did not observe My commandments properly. It then says: 'But this is the covenant that I will make with the House of Israel after those days', i.e., after that Exile; 'I will put My law in their inward parts and in their heart will I write it'. What I wrote for their ancestors on tablets of stone, I now write on the tablet of their heart, where it will be inscribed and not forgotten. Next it says: 'I will be their God and they shall be My people, and they shall teach no more every man his neighbour and every man his brother, saying, know the Lord—for they shall know Me from the least of them unto the greatest of them, saith the Lord, for I will forgive their iniquity and their sins will I remember no more'.

The general rule for all this consolation is that God causes evil to perish from this world, and all believers will have faith in Him from their childhood to their old age—and God will forgive all former iniquities from the time of Adam onwards and will make good man's inclination which was *ab initio* bad. This is explained differently by Ezekiel, who says (xxxvi. 26–27): 'A new heart also will I give you and a new spirit will I put within you; and I will take away the stony heart out of your flesh and I will give you a heart of flesh; and I will put My spirit within you and cause you to walk in My statutes and ye shall keep My judgments and do them'. In the first verse He gives you a new heart and a new spirit —two things, heart and spirit, which previously were possessed in a different form and manner. He explains the form of the old heart which He removes from their flesh and calls it a stone, as it says: 'I will take away the stony heart out of your flesh.'

How are the hearts of men in this world like stone? A man does not have to be shown how to use his limbs; he uses them naturally in the manner in which they were created. For example: God made the foot for walking, the hand for grasping, the ear for hearing, the eye for seeing, and the heart for understanding. Every limb was created to benefit man in a certain way and does so whenever man so wills. None of the limbs needs to be trained— except the human heart which cannot perform its function unless it is guided and trained, and from that training it acquires the power to understand—and if you do not train it, it is incapable of directing itself and the other bodily functions dependent on it. The spirit it acquires can be good or evil and the heart acts accordingly. In this respect the heart is like a stone, which has no power to move from its place or change its form and man moves it and shapes it according to his will. Similarly the heart has no power to direct or influence the spirit—but will act as man directs and trains it—unlike the other limbs, for they from the outset control their faculties without assistance. That is why the heart resembles and is called a stone. But when God trains it as the other limbs which control their faculties, it no longer resembles a stone, and He calls it flesh similar to the other limbs, as it says 'I will give you a heart of flesh'.

It does not mention the form of the old spirit, which is removed and replaced with a new spirit—as it mentions the nature of the old heart which it calls 'stone'—because the spirit acquired by the heart in this world did not exist in it at the time of its creation but came from without and is acquired by teaching and training. You can say that it existed potentially, and that it is actualized by training and education; and that, at the time of redemption, God brings out the spirit, which existed potentially in the hearts of His people for good or for evil, and He actualizes it and brings it out solely for good. As it says 'I will bring My spirit within you', i.e., My good and upright spirit. The heart will control that spirit as is the case with the other limbs and it will not have to be trained and taught as was the case hitherto.

It says 'And I will cause you to walk in My statutes and ye shall keep My judgments and do them'—the fear and worship of God and all good conduct which existed potentially will now be implanted by God in their hearts and will not be left to human decision, as was the case previously. And all who will be in the world at that time—namely Israel and all associated with them, as we have learned above—will be united in faith and fear and they will observe all the commandments enshrined in their hearts and uttered by their mouth, and all the world will be upright. The proof of it is clear to all who understand the Torah, as it is written 'Thou shalt love thy neighbour as thyself' (Leviticus xix. 18)—this commandment will be observed by all on earth at the time of salvation. And if everyone in the world will be loving his neighbour, as he loves himself, then jealousy, hatred and covetousness will disappear from the world—and these are the causes of war and slaughter. Therefore the Bible tells about messianic times (Isaiah ii. 4): 'And you shall beat your swords into ploughshares and your spears to pruning-hooks, nation shall not lift up sword against nation'. This verse alone warns against five negative commandments—viz., the last five of the Ten Commandments.

I conclude by saying that we see from the Torah that God strengthens the hearts of His people to believe in Him, know His way, and firmly maintain the Torah throughout their life. By this, all hatred, rivalry and jealousy will be ended and when these good qualities are recognized, they will despise this world and all its affairs. So you will see that he who despises the world and removes himself from its preoccupations draws closer to the ways of God and deserves a good life. As one of them said, 'If you change life to love of life you will acquire life' or, in other words, despise the world for the glory of the Lord of the world and you will rule the world. You see from here that a man can acquire the world for very little and it is easy to do and involves no effort; it is a question of suppressing your desires so that you should hate the vain pleasures of this world, which cause exertion and sorrow. In this way you will free yourself from the burden of this world and go out from Exile and attain salvation and the Kingdom of God. He who considers the good and desirable things of this world will find many corresponding loathsome evils. He will not enjoy the good, except for the object of removing the evil. He will eat and drink only to remove hunger and thirst, and if out of greed he partakes of more than is essential, he brings evil and sickness to his body. That is why the individuals separated unto God eat whatever is to hand, not for the sake of its taste, but to prevent hunger, and they wear clothes so as not to be harmed by the cold, and it makes no difference whether they are of wool or linen; and those who follow their path, will attain their superiority. He who considers this explanation of the verse will be greatly benefited therefrom, as it says (Ecclesiastes v. 11): 'The sleep of a labouring man is sweet, whether he eat little or much; but the fullness of the rich will not suffer him to sleep'.

May God in His many mercies enable me to understand the proper fear of Him, to comprehend the path of faith, to maintain the love of Him, to understand His divinity, to rely on His Torah, and to trust in His salvation. And may we be worthy of His kindness and goodness, as it says (Psalms xxxii. 10): 'He that trusteth in the Lord, mercy shall compass him about'.

'The Book of the Meditation' is completed. Praise to God on High. Blessed be He that giveth the weary strength, and for those that are weak increaseth power.

Blessed is the writer. Blessed is the reader. Be strong.